Hot Like Fire

Sexy Tales in Philadelphia

by

Leah Lockett Harris

Disclaimer

This book is a work of fiction. Names, characters, businesses, individuals, places, events, organizations, locales, establishment and incidents are either a product of the author's imagination or are used fictitiously.

Any resemblance, to actual businesses, individuals, places, events, organizations, locales, establishment or incidents are either a product of the author's imagination, purely coincidental or used to give the reader a sense of reality and authenticity.

The mention of any businesses, individuals, places, events, organizations, locales, and establishments in this fictitious document is not to be misconstrued as fact, intent of fact, misrepresentation or liable.

****

All Rights Reserved

Published by Leah Lockett Harris for LLH Publishing, LLC

Edited by Leah Lockett Harris

Copyright © 2007 by Leah Lockett Harris

Distribution by LuLu.com

ISBN 978-0-6151-5264-6

This book may not be reproduced in whole or part by mimeograph or any other means, without permission of the author.

Please direct all question and comments to
LeahLockettHarris@yahoo.com

Table of Contents

1. Photographs — 3
2. Gold Digger — 22
3. Candy Man — 45
4. Hood Boy — 69
5. The Stand Up - Part One — 86
6. The Stand Up - Part Two — 101
7. The Substitute — 119
8. Train Ride — 155
9. Therapy — 158
10. The Party — 174

Photographs

Well, well, well if it isn't Armand Parker, Mr. Photographer extraordinaire! Mia said entering Armand's new East Falls studio, her raincoat and umbrella dripping with rainwater.

"Mia Tallington!" Armand replied with his arms outstretched embracing his longtime friend with a hearty hug and kiss. "Baby girl you look amazing." He said, taking her in.

Mia took the compliment graciously, silently thanking her yoga instructor. "You don't look too shabby yourself Mia answered sincerely. Armand with all his forty-two years could easily be mistaken for a man almost half his age. Not including the few gray hairs that were creeping up his temples he could definitely pass for a man in his late twenties.

Armand took Mia's coat and umbrella and handed her a glass of wine. He paused just for a moment admiring the way her black dress hugged her smooth curves, how her plunging neckline showed off all of her bounty. "I'm glad you could make it Mia, I really hope you like this."

"I'll like anything you do Armand, you know that." Armand blushed and gave her one of his signature brilliant smiles. Mia found her self once again lost in the brightness just as she had been so many years ago 'still as fine as ever' she thought. "What has it been ten, eleven years since we've stood face to face?"

"Yeah, just about." Armand replied placing his hand at the small of her back guiding her down the hall to his exhibit room. "Thank God for cell phones and email, huh?"

Mia's shoulder length dark hair brushed past Armand's nose as she turned her head to smile at him; the familiar scent of vanilla and patchouli filled his senses, momentarily taking him back to the days when his fingers ran freely through those soft curls.

I guess we got away from each other huh?" Mia said not missing the look of melancholy in Armand's eyes.

"More like we were forced to be." At Armand's comment the two of them were silent for a moment, both caught up in remembering the pain of that night. "But hey," He said realizing their trip down memory lane was beginning to take them to a somber place. "Were here together tonight, guess you can't keep good friends away from each other for too long."

'Friends' Mia thought dryly, there was a time when she would have dropped any and everything just to be with this man, the fact that they considered themselves only friends now was a sad fact, in itself.

Armand instantly tuned into her melancholy mood and quickly jumped in to free her from it, "Oh Mia girl, give me a hug." Armand said holding her tightly in his arms. He meant for the gesture to be comforting, but found himself becoming instantly aroused from being so close to her. Just having his arms around her shoulders had him remembering those many nights, always after midnight when he would be wrapped in the comfort of he warm embrace. He knew every curve of her beautiful body every dip; every luscious bend and he knew better than anyone how to please her. Blinking away his reverie, he cleared his throat. "Well, enough about that now."

Mia had a harder time diverting her thoughts away from the past. She had been in what was to her a loveless marriage for over ten years, and just by chance discovered that Armand was the 'it' that was missing from her monotonous life for so long, she reveled in the sensual moments where he freed her from the prison of a life she was too afraid to walk away from and from her prisoner…namely Gavin.

Gavin, her husband was a high-ranking Philadelphia narcotics detective, he was excellent at what he did professionally, but lacked seriously in the husband department. To say he was neglectful as a husband was putting it lightly, most of the time Gavin was downright vindictive and mean to Mia. Perhaps it was so many years on the force that made him that way; perhaps he'd been that way all along. To him Mia was simply her trophy wife, the pretty young thing fifteen years his junior that he kept to prove to his cronies he still had it as a man. It was beside the fact that both he and Mia knew he didn't.

In fact, Mia doubted Gavin ever really loved her and as for making love to her…well forget it. Back when he was still able to get it up he was all thumbs in bed. A night of making love with him would consist of three minutes of him grunting and pushing until he howled from his own sweaty satisfaction, she herself got nothing out of being with him. Simply put she was his possession and that's how he treated her.

Mia wondered how she ever let Gavin fool her into marriage in the first place. Perhaps being alone with no family made her an easy target for him. With a lot of effort she finally pulled herself away from those bitter thoughts about her past; 'life is different now,' she tried to remind herself.

"Sooo, Armand what is this exhibit called?" This was the first she was able to see in person for some time, before now she'd only been able to view his work in magazine's and the occasional email he'd sent her from one or another amazing place he'd traveled around the world.

"Piercing Midnight" Armand replied and as soon as he did a flush of heat ran down into Mia's belly. Midnight was when all their secret meetings would take place. All those delicious escapes, that didn't feel like she was escaping at all. Being with Armand felt like she was home. With him she felt free to be the woman she was meant to be, exotic, erotic, and sometimes downright nasty if she wanted to be. She and Armand spent dozens of nights exploring every sexual fantasy and position they could imagine.

"Oh," was all that issued from her mouth feeling that same rush of excitement that standing so close to Armand gave her eleven years ago. Then she chided herself so being so foolish. Chances are Armand put all of that behind him a long time ago. Just because she wasn't' able to forget him didn't mean he felt the same way. Perhaps 'Piercing Midnight' was just the theme for the evening. After all the invitation did read Philadelphia After Midnight. "Silly" she said, not meaning to say it aloud.

"What's silly, Mia", Armand asked looking at her intently.

"Oh, nothing. It's just um...I just." Mia said smiling nervously. Not knowing what else to say she quickly drowned her glass of chardonnay. How could she tell him

4

that just the mention of Midnight transported her immediately back to his bed so many years before, and as if it was only moments before she could still feel him slowly and deliberately stroking himself inside of her, deeper and deeper as she begged for more. After all this time, she was still feeling him, tasting him, craving him.

"Wow," Armand said laughing. "Thirsty huh lady, would you like another."

Mia blushed feeling warm from the rush of wine inside her, "that would probably be a good idea." Mia said hoping the wine would help steady her nerves. She wouldn't have guessed in a million years she would react this way just from being close to Armand again. Sipping on the fresh glass, her eyes tried to avoid Armand's. Being 'just friends' was a whole lot easier for her through emails than it was in person.

As Armand poured himself a glass of wine, Mia forced herself to calm down 'easy girl, stop acting foolish' she told herself hoping something inside her would listen. Forcing a casual smile she said, "So Armand it's already midnight now, what time are your other guest arriving?"

"Everyone I invited is already here." He replied coyly.

Mia glanced around the room, it was definitely set for an evening of entertaining, from the soft lights, to the even softer jazz piping through his Bose sound system. There were snacks and cheeses on the marble bar and several bottles of wine were lined up ready to be uncorked. He put a whole lot of effort into an evening that was just intended for two 'old friends' to catch up on old times. She thought about all the detail he put into this evening, the elaborate invitation with raised lettering, the car that swung by at eleven thirty to pick her up, this gallery done up so nicely, all of this just for her?

She looked around the room and saw at least a dozen easels covered in white cloth with spotlights focused on each of them. What was behind them was beyond her, but knowing it was intended for her eyes only gave her the jitters, she suddenly felt nervous. Mia raised her glass to her lips, and quickly forced down another swallow.

Armand took her glass and his and set them on the marble wet bar. "Shall we get started?" He said taking her hand approaching the first canvassed easel.

Mia didn't realize she'd been holding her breath until a sigh of relief escaped her lips when Armand uncovered the first photograph. Mia wasn't sure what she expected to see but the picture of Boathouse Row at night with the luminous moon gliding over the Schuylkill River was far from anything her jumbled mind was imagining.

"Oh Armand, this is wonderful, the way you captured the moonlight dappling across the water makes Boat house row appear almost ethereal. It's eerie and graceful at the same time."

'I call it 'Lonely with a Promise'. Armand replied.

"Exactly," Mia said enthusiastically, "It's like the moment, before the moment, you know what I mean?"

"Ahh Mia, that's one of the things I so deeply treasure about you baby girl. You've always had a way of putting what I feel into words that make sense. Like you see my vision, but even better you can explain it."

Mia blushed at his compliment, and he was right, she could always sense and understand what it was that Armand was feeling, which is probably what made their lovemaking so purposeful, so intense.

The next few photos were of scenes from around Philadelphia, all late at night with the luminous glow of the moon painting each scene with melancholy light. As Armand uncovered each picture, Mia realized she hadn't been as silly as she first thought. It took her a while but when she finally put the pieces together she was awestruck. Each picture depicted moments the two of them shared together. Without saying a word she backtracked to the first picture and the next. The sequence was clearly there, and Armand did miss her, these photos proved it. It must have taken him weeks to retrace all the places they'd been together, all the moments of their secret relationship. "Oh Armand," was all she could say.

Their first night, the night they met was "Lonely with Promise". After a night of arguing with Gavin, Mia waited for him to leave for his shift at the precinct and then decided to take a drive to blow off some steam. That night, like many other nights, she felt trapped and alone in her marriage. Mia was once again contemplating leaving Gavin, but she knew he'd do as he always did, track her down and force her to come back home with him.

Depressed, she let her car wind idly through Fairmount Park as Luther Vandross sang beautiful but sad songs to her through her radio. It was chance that led her to MLK Drive. Something, she wasn't sure what, made her stop and speak to the lonesome photographer taking pictures late at night of Boat House Row. Perhaps it was because he looked as lonely as she felt. Pulling her car up onto the narrow slip of grass that separated the road from the glistening river, she parked alongside his truck. Stepping out of her car without any sense of fear Mia walked over and joined him by his vehicle.

'Desperate souls joined' is what came to mind when she recalled how happy he seemed to be when he realized that she was there.

Mia looked the stranger over, he was tall and nicely fit, with a complexion that reminded her of caramel being drizzled over vanilla ice cream, his hair closely cut flowed in neatly groomed waves against his head. His features were so fine that he looked almost feminine with his huge deep brown eyes, lengthy eye lashes and a sculpted nose; only his square jaw and slightly larger than normal ears belied his masculinity. His over sized shirt and loose fitting jeans did nothing to hide his broad back, trim waist and sexy ass, none of which Gavin's dumpy physique could boast. 'He's perfect,' she thought.

Their meeting started off pleasant enough, Armand appeared to be truly grateful to have someone there to talk to and so was she. As it turned out Armand wasn't only gorgeous, he was intelligent and insightful. She enjoyed his take on everything. Through his eyes she saw everything around them in a whole new light. He never asked her why she was out there so late at night, he simply drew her in to his work, she helped him position his camera while he explained his purpose for capturing the landmark in a light that no one had ever seen it before.

Mia grateful to have something other than Gavin and her marriage to think about became fully engrossed in conversation with Armand. Despite herself she realized she'd begun flirting with Armand and he for his part responded by flirting with her in return. For the first time in years she felt young, attractive, free.

A little joke or pleasant comment from Mia would be rewarded by Armand's beautiful smile. When Armand stood behind her and showed her how to put the camera in focus, her ass naturally leaned back against him, letting him know that conversation was nice but she had other things in mind.

Before either of them knew what was happening the two of them were passionately kissing in the back of his truck. Only the camera stood on it's tripod taking automatic timed pictures of the lighted boathouses. Mia and Armand twisted feverously in each other's embrace, Armand only pausing long enough to slide his condom on.

Armand rode her, the dark chocolate of her skin swirling deliciously with the caramel of his. This stranger seemed intent on satisfying her as much as he humanly could, and he did one world-shaking orgasm after another. When he finally allowed himself to release, he did so holding her tightly as he intensely whispered curses in her ears.

By the time the sun began to rise over the Art Museum, Mia realized she and her new lover hadn't even exchanged first names, but she felt as if she knew everything she ever needed to know about this man; simply put he was everything she ever wanted in a man. Learning his name as they kissed their first goodbye only served to put a label on what she thought of as pure perfection.

By the time Gavin returned home at eight that morning, Mia was tucked back in her bed with Armand's telephone number and address secreted in the bottom of her nightstand drawer.

Recalling that night now Mia couldn't believe how reckless she had been, anything could have happened to her, worst of all Armand could have been dangerous. In retrospect she knew she had taken quite a chance, but she never regretted it. She realized Armand was watching her waiting for a response from her before he uncovered the next photograph. "They're about us aren't they?"

"Yes they are, do you want to see more?" Armand asked her hoping she would say yes.

"All of them?" Mia wanted to know.

"All of them and they get more…intense. Do you want to see the rest?"

"Yeah, I do." Mia said with a smile and Armand's heart leaped when she did. There was so much he wanted to say to her, so many moments he wanted to remind her of. Like old the cliché 'a picture is worth a thousand words' he decided to let the pictures do the talking for him. He wanted nothing more than for this night to end with them picking up where they left off so many years ago but he needed to know that she wanted it too.

It pained him to think of all of the time that was wasted all of the moment that were lost because he was forced to leave her just to save his life and hers.

When he pulled back the next cover, Mia's breath drew in with a gasp. This picture wasn't of just places they'd been together, but of the two of them. Mia immediately recognized the curve of her back arching over Armand's body, the muscles of her tight body pulled and taut from her intense deliberate movements, her thighs tightly clenched around his hips securing him in place as she rode him. Black sheets were wrapped and tangled all around their arms and legs, as caught up as they were in their passion.

The camera that took this picture must have been angled above them for her mess of soft curls completely covered his face. But Mia knew without even seeing that Armand was blindfolded, her idea. His hands were tied together by a single red scarf, which was secured to the frame of his wrought iron bed. This again was her idea.

"When did you, I mean how…" was all that she could form her lips to say. The answer to her question of course was obvious, Armand was first and foremost a photographer, and he captured everything on film. It should have been no surprise to her that he would secretly photograph the two of them together as well.

She remembered that night well, she and Armand had been seeing each other for weeks by then, and unless he was away on business the two of them were together basically every night. That night she arrived at his loft wearing only an over coat and red stiletto heels and carrying a small leather bag filled with tricks. When Armand realized she was naked underneath her coat he reached out to remove it, when he did his hands met the strike of her small whip that she'd pulled from her bag. Smiling he backed away from her towards his bed.

He let Mia tie him up, blindfold him tease him, punish him gently with her whip till he begged for her. Before she would give in to him she ground herself on every part of his body that she could, making herself come on his legs, his thighs, even his toes. Leaving behind a trail of wet patches from her little orgasms. Then she straddled his face and rode his tongue until her juices flowed down his chin, all the while cursing under her breath telling him what good sex slave he was being.

Mia lowered her face and returned the favor daring Armand to move; if he did he was met with a strike from her whip. When she felt him close to coming, she raised herself from his bed and walked away torturing him. After he'd become completely soft she returned; this time with a bowlful of ice; pleasing and torturing him until he exploded in her mouth like a geyser.

By the time his camera took this picture she was again on top of him greedily filling her wet hole with his hardness.

Mia remembered how sexy and powerful she felt that night, how willing Armand was to let her take complete control.

Not many nights after he turned the tables on her. blindfolded, he took her completely naked, except for the red stiletto heels, out onto the balcony of his loft, tying her to the railing, taking her over and over again in the cool summer air until her knees were weak from standing. She relished being his submissive as much as being his mistress and thinking about it now so many years later had her wanting him even more.

"More" escaped her mouth in a raspy voice she didn't recognize; still she wasn't prepared for what she saw next.

Mia could barely make out the moonlit images but she knew what they were. There was one night that the two of them stopped off for drinks at an obscure Samson Street bar, after several drinks and some serious petting in the darkened corner of the bar, they decided to continue the evening at Armand's loft. Several Cosmopolitans later, they walked down the darkened alley of Samson Street heading back towards Armand's truck, halfway there he grabbed her by the hand and gently pushed her against the cool brick wall. Armand's insistent kisses drove her crazy and when he told her that he had to have her right then, right there, she hungrily purred out yes.

Armand dove into her, roughly hiking her skirt above her hips, dropping his pants and taking her there in the shadows. Mia remembered how forceful he'd been almost ripping her clothes off then savagely thrusting inside her. As she bit down on his shoulder he whispered in her ear telling her in how good it felt to be inside her. Armand lifted her higher wrapping her legs around his hips.

Mia still recalled the cool roughness of the brick wall scratching the tender skin of her behind while he thrust himself deeper and deeper inside of her. He came hard, once again whispering soft curses in her ears. Then tenderly as he had been forceful dropped to his knees and tasted her until she cried out in satisfaction. That was when his timer took this shot, of him with his face buried between her spread legs, her fingers clasped behind his head, her face contorted in ecstasy. Only the moon casting over them provided enough light for the camera to capture them.

"I left the camera on automatic when we left for the bar, I set it to take a shot every ten minutes, by the time you and I had left I'd gotten dozens of other frames but none of them were quite like this." Armand said aloud, silently hoping she wasn't pissed.

"No…how could they be." Mia said absently, feeling both the wine and the slow pulsation of arousal between her legs. Thinking back she thought that moment was just them being spontaneous, be he'd planned all of it, their making love right there in the alley was his idea all along. She knew should be upset with him, for taking these pictures without her permission…but she wasn't. Mia was turned on and hungrier for Armand than she'd ever been.

Mia went around the room uncovering the last few pictures on her own. Armand stood back and let his work speak for itself. There were pictures of them in the shower, in bed, on the floor, in the park, everywhere he could set up a camera he had images of them making love.

"Why didn't you ever tell me you had these?" Mia said pacing back and forth between pictures mesmerized at how raw and sensual each on was.

"Are you upset with me?" Armand said holding his breath in hoping for life she wasn't.

"No…actually, I'm kind of turned on to see us captured this way, we were so sensual…so real."

"That's what I've always thought, I kept them with me always, they were my mementos from the happiest time of my life. The only time I'd ever been in love." The words poured from Armand's mouth so purely Mia thought her heart would melt right there.

"Why didn't you ever tell me about them?" Armand must have known seeing these pictures would have made her even hotter for him.

"I'd planned to that night ..." He wanted to tell her it was also the night he planned to ask her to leave Gavin for him, the night he planned to tell her he loved her, but decided against it.

"What stopped you?" Mia said facing him, and as soon as she did the look on his face gave her, her answer. "Oh, Armand I'm sorry!"

It was that night their last night, Gavin had eventually caught on to the fact that Mia was having an affair. Mia guessed to some he would have been viewed as the injured party, after all Armand had been sleeping around with his wife. And she supposed some would perhaps come to Gavin's defense, justify his actions that night, But to Mia it was just more of Gavin's cruelty…he seemed to enjoy that night way too much.

By now they'd been seeing each other for close to five months, Mia was as much at home at Armand's loft as she was in the home she shared with Gavin, even more so. Mia wasn't sure what gave her away. Perhaps she was happy too often, which Gavin despised or maybe he realized he was losing his control. Mia no longer cared what Gavin thought or did. She knew no matter how bad the argument was, how horrible the sex was or how mean Gavin was to her, everything would be better a soon a she was in Armand's arms again. And as careful as she thought she was being somehow she led Gavin to Armand's place. In the midst of them in each other's embrace, the two of them were startled one night at the sound of Armand's loft door being kicked in.

It was Gavin flanked by two of the cops from his precinct. Without saying a word he brutally dragged her out of the bed by her hair, and as two of his flunkies beat poor Armand to a pulp Gavin hovered over her, his knee in her chest forcing her to watch. When the nightmare was finally over Gavin uttered a single threat to Armand before dragging Mia away. "See her again and you both die."

Mia not sure if Armand was even conscious tried to run to him just to be met with a back handed slap from Gavin. Mia fell to the floor with a thud; unconcerned Gavin dragged her out of Armand's loft as if she was little more than a rag doll. When they got home Gavin lost it, he promised to hunt Armand down and kill him like a dog if she ever tried to contact him again. Mia considered getting help, but whom would she turn to, Gavin was the police and who would have sympathy for her...no one.

As angry as Mia was she was afraid too, not of what Gavin would do to her but of what he might do to Armand. For months he kept a close eye on her, posting one of his flunkies outside the house whenever he had to be away. Despite her fear of Gavin she attempted to locate Armand, at least let him know she was sorry. Several months went by with no word from him at all. Mia couldn't blame him if he never wanted to speak to her again.

It wasn't until month later did she get an email from Japan, the email address was from an "ichibonsansai". Not knowing who it was she almost deleted the email. On a hunch she opened it, it was an advertisement for a photography exhibit taking place in Tokyo that weekend. The picture on the ad showed a Geisha with her makeup half on, half off. Armand had taught her so much about light and texture that she knew from the look of the photograph that it was from him and sent a message saying only, 'I'm okay'.

Emails came in from all over the world; Europe, Australia, Africa, South America. That's how it continued for several years. Eventually Gavin let up on her, he was less argumentative and mean, and he'd stopped threatening her and the cops were no longer being posted outside her home. Armand would let her know where he'd been through pictures and brief emails, but he never came close to Philly in all that time.

By the time he settled in LA they were chatting briefly online, the occasional call to her job surprised and delighted her. Every time she could Mia told Armand how sorry she was, how much she missed him.

Late one fall, Gavin and his two cronies turned up murdered in a drug investigation gone wrong. Mia was more relieved, than distraught and that in itself made her sad. Despite their unhappy marriage she didn't wish her husband dead she would have preferred to have just gotten away from him.

It was less than a year later when Armand called to tell her he was putting down roots again in Philadelphia. Mia delighted with the news couldn't wait to see him. That's what brought her to this night these moments after midnight learning that he missed her as much as she missed him.

"It's ok, Mia…that was a long time ago." He said taking her into his arms, 'A lifetime ago', he thought. That night when Mia's husband and those assholes broke into his apartment, they messed him up pretty good. Three broken ribs, a bruised spleen and a fractured jaw good. He'd spent weeks in the hospital checked in under an alias, warding off questions of what had happened to him.

When he was discharged he didn't even return to his loft, after phoning a friend in Japan he was on a flight that morning without looking back. From the moment he arrived he wanted to contact Mia, but he needed to be careful; he was out of harm's way but she wasn't.

Armand had all the items from his place packed up and sent to him, among them was the film from the camera that he had perched over his bookshelf to capture more intimate moment of he and Mia. He had to admit, he was a voyeur by nature, which is why he chose his profession in the first place. Seeing the honesty and sincerity on Mia's face in shots she didn't even know she was taking told him more about the way she felt for him than any of the words she could say. It was this last roll of film that he had to develop not because he wanted to see himself being brutally beaten, but because he needed those pictures, each and every one of them to fuel his plan to get revenge.

From what Armand knew of Gavin, he was an arrogant shortsighted asshole. Yeah, he muscled his way into his home and roughed him up and for what? His wife was still in love with another man. Had he been a man and kept his wife happy she would have never been out driving in the middle of the night for the two of them to have met. He was able to keep Mia all of those years not because she wanted him, but because she was afraid of him.

Armand went on with his life, and his career as a photographer boomed, but he never for a moment forgot what he owed Gavin and his goons. He also kept in touch with Mia just so she knew she wasn't forgotten. He knew it would be some time before he could get her back but Armand was going to get his woman back.

By the time he returned to the states Armand had made some interesting contacts back home in Philly, in no time and for less than a few thousand dollars his plan was in place. Once he had the ball rolling, it was nothing for him to catch the red eye into Newark, New Jersey, drive down to Philly in a rented car, pick up the bag that was waiting for him in a bus station locker and handle his business. His plan was seamless, well thought out and calculated.

Looking at Mia now he realized it was worth it, he'd finally gotten his revenge and his woman. When he tracked Gavin's whereabouts, without hesitation he pulled out the automatic rifle in his bag, and with pleasure gunned all three of them down just blocks away from the precinct. In not time at all Armand was on a flight back to LA. The press reported it was due to a drug bust that had gone bad. He paid only a few hundred dollars to have that tip called in to a news station.

'Photographs' Armand thought to himself, there were so many he'd destroyed, so many he'd never let Mia see, like the bullet ridden body of Gavin sitting inside his unmarked police car next to a box of unopened donuts; of his flunkies just a few feet away already dead with steam rising from their still warm bodies on the ground. The moonlight at midnight was casting a sickish glare on Gavin's lifeless face. The shocked expression of him recognizing Armand seconds before he perished, frozen forever in place.

"You know what I'd like to do Mia?" Armand was feeling pretty good standing here so close to the woman he's craved for so many years. Instinctively he pulled her into his arms.

Mia blushed after accepting Armand's long passionate kiss, yeah she still wanted him, "what's that baby?" she replied her voice breathy…erotic.

"Take you back to my place, where we can take some pictures."

Mia looked long into Armand's eyes, her belly filled with wanting her thighs nervous with desire. "Is your camera here, Armand?"

Armand smiled into Mia's eyes, she'd already begun sliding out of her dress, her eyes never breaking his gaze. "Yeah, why?"

"Because I don't I think I can wait till we get to your place." Mia said sliding out of her bra.

"You want it now baby?" Armand asked setting his camera up on its tripod.

"Mmm hmm, I want it now." Mia said standing now wearing nothing but her knee length black leather boots.

Armand quickly removed his shirt, as Mia tugged on the zipper of his pants. As the camera's shutter clicked away catching dozens of frames of them falling to the floor, feeling, tasting, teasing, exploring.

Click.

"Mmm." Armand moaned as his hands slid down the length of her

Click…click…click.

"Fuck me." Mia whispered moving her hips against the fingers now sliding in and out of her wetness.

Click…click…click…click…click.

"Yes." Armand said as her thighs opened up for him as he moved himself deeper inside.

Click…click…click…click.

"Harder!" Mia commanded Armand as they rocked covered in sweat.

Click…click

Click.

The camera had almost run out of film by the time Armand felt himself about to explode inside Mia. Mia sensing him arched her hips forward sliding him in deeper than before feeling her own pressure build as he bounced against her.

They both cried out loud screaming each other's names as they came. Armand embraced Mia tightly until her shudders stopped and she collapsed satisfied in his arms.

She was back…Mia was finally his woman again.

Click.

Gold Digger

"**Oh God Tara,** I hate him!" Kellie spat in frustration, the midnight sky illuminating their faces as the two women sat twenty-nine stories up on Tara's penthouse balcony, observing the hustle and bustle of Delaware Avenue or Christopher Columbus Boulevard, the name that the historic riverfront avenue had been changed to. The pulsating nightlife to their right and to their left was the quiet serenity of the Delaware River and the water front view of Camden, New Jersey.

Tara said nothing sipping on her beer, watching as some ant sized cars flowed in and out of Rock Lobster and Dave and Buster's. From her vantage point up here in her water front condo she could enjoy the sights of Philadelphia's nightlife without being in it. With binoculars, she could even see as far as South Philly clearly.

Tara regarded Kellie in the darkness, a quirky young model, miles from her California State home. The fact they'd become friends was an oddity in itself. She and Kellie couldn't be more different. But now, especially after her roommate Jada had moved out, she welcomed Kellie's visits. She and Kellie had been friendly for a little over four months now, maybe five and this was Kellie's fourth late night visit to Tara's apartment. Once again she'd had a major fight with her boyfriend Covington.

"I mean I know he's an Aries," Kellie continued "but does he has to turn everything into a fucking competition?" Tara said spilling some of her Corona Light on her white t-shirt. "I mean if I say white, he'll automatically say black, then do everything in his power to prove he's the hell right! And I'm not talking about one argument; nooo, he'll make that shit last for days just to make his point. Once he kicked me out of his car in the middle of nowhere just because I wouldn't agree that Manhattan clam chowder was better than the New England kind…fucking idiot!"

"Mmm hmm" was all that Tara said, when Kellie was on a tirade, she learned it was best just to let her finish.

"And I'm tired as hell of him telling me how stupid I am when I have a higher IQ then he does. Just because he's older does not make him smarter! I swear I'm about five second from moving my ass back to Santa Barbara."

Tara took a sip from her bottle of beer, 'it's not healthy," she said.

"What?"

"I said it's not healthy."

"What's not healthy?"

Tara puffed her cheeks and blew softly in mild exasperation; she'd been listening to Kellie's tirade for well over an hour now. "How long have the two of you been together?" Tara of course knew the answer, but she had a point to make.

"Ten months, it'll be a year in September."

"And how old are you?' Tara knew the answer to that as well.

"Twenty three."

"And how old his he?"

"Forty eight…" Kellie said not understanding what she was getting at.

"How often do you two fight like this?"

"Well lately almost every fucking day, but that's because he's an asshole!"

"Why do you do this to yourself Kel? Why not just move on?" Tara said, "I mean if he makes you so unhappy, why not leave him, maybe find someone new…or better yet be on your own for a while."

Kellie's face twisted as if she'd suddenly felt a quick pain, "Yeah right," Kellie said mashing her cigarette butt in Tara's Lenox crystal ashtray. "I'm not like you Tara, I'd need help to afford all this." Waving her hands around.

'This' was Tara's two thousand square foot luxury apartment just north of Penn's Landing situated right on the Delaware River. Her high rise home boasted a master suite, two additional bedrooms, three baths one with a four person Jacuzzi, a gourmet kitchen with marble counter tops, two gas fireplaces, hardwood floors, custom cabinetry throughout and a balcony with an exceptional view of the Philadelphia sky line. On top of that Tara's place had been professionally decorated and with the help of her housekeeper it stayed magazine layout ready at all times. The place Kellie shared with her boyfriend eight flights down wasn't nearly as opulent, but it was still luxurious.

"I couldn't always afford this either Kel, but that didn't mean I thought I should put up with bullshit everyday when I couldn't…I just lived more simple."

Kellie shifted uncomfortably in Tara's outdoor chair. "Yeah well I guess you couldn't miss what you never had, but I on the other hand like living this way. I've gotten used to the luxury, I'm not ready to leave it all."

Tara rolled her eyes in the darkness, "So you'd rather kiss his ass then struggle on your own for a minute?"

Kellie wrinkled up her nose, "I'm not saying that…" 'It's what I know' Kellie thought to herself. Kellie was raised to think of men as income. She thought about her mother Rachel's personal mantra, 'you got to use what you got to get what you want'.

Rachel and Kellie's two aunts Elizabeth and Kathleen; all fair skinned redheads lived their lives by that credo. All three party girls were blessed with Irish beauty, ghetto booty, a love for black men and a penchant for luxurious living.

What better trappings for newly rich young athletes to fall for then three gorgeous white girls who couldn't get enough of them. Rachel stuck to basketball players, while her sisters preferred the NFL.

Though their marriages didn't last, the alimony and years of child support did. Now that she and her cousins were grown and scattered about the country, the three of them lived well together in a house they all purchased with their ex-husband money back in Santa Barbara.

Kelly thought about her own father, a legendary NBA basketball player, he was currently on his fourth wife now, a blonde named Suzette. After her parents divorced when she was not even two years old, she may have seen him in person two times tops after that. But Rachel didn't seem to mind that her child was all but fatherless, as long as his ample child support checks arrived regularly.

Not that Kellie wanted to go down that road, but if her needs called for it, then well…*I ain't saying she's a gold digger* played silently in Kellie's head.

"If you gave yourself some time, I bet you'd be affording a place like this before you know it. I mean look at you, already your modeling career is taking off."

"And in the meantime do what? Go back to sharing an apartment with three or four other girls…I don't think so."

"At least you'd have some peace of mind."

"Yeah, and I'd be stuck spending all my time guarding my damn wardrobe from thieving roommates. Doesn't sound like a plan to me."

"But staying with an older man that belittles you, cusses and argues with you… just 'cause he's willing to foot the bill is your plan huh?"

"C'mon Tara you're acting like you've never had to rely on a Big Daddy to help you out at some point." Kellie said sucking her teeth; she couldn't understand why Tara was being so judgmental.

"Me…actually no. I set my sights on what I wanted then I worked for it." Tara thought about all the years of grueling hours she put in at the station long before they finally gave her a show.

She like her competition Wendy Williams battled their way onto the airwaves. Now she was the reigning queen of the morning radio and her syndicated satellite show was among the top ten in the country. Her career along with some shrewd investments had her rather wealthy for her thirty-four years.

"You've never had a older dude, a sugar daddy help you out a little?" That thought was beyond Kellie's comprehension.

"Hah!" Tara laughed. "The only daddy I've ever had was my dead beat one."

Kellie peered at Tara over the rim of her beer bottle and wondered for a moment. True, Tara was fiercely independent and she admired that about her, but sometimes she took it a little too far. Sure, Tara was rich now, but even she admitted that wasn't always the case. Getting a little help from the men in your life never hurt anyone…most women were hip to that.

Except for maybe a lesbo. Now that she thought about it, she'd never seen Tara with any man. Sure she'd heard rumors that Tara had once been engaged, but to who, and why hadn't he been replaced yet? Before she even considered her words Kellie blurted out, "Are you a lesbian Tara"?

Tara's laugh caught in her throat this time "Me, hah! No…not really."

'What was that supposed to mean?' Kellie wondered to herself. "Not really, usually means yes." Kellie said teasingly.

Now it was Tara's turn to shift uncomfortably. "I mean...I've had relationships."

"With who?" Kellie asked, grateful the focus of the conversation was off of her for a minute.

"With people." Tara responded.

"Stop playing Tara, male or female people?" Kellie asked. This was getting good she thought.

Tara chewed the inside of her cheek; if she answered that question truthfully, she knew it would open a whole can of worms. 'What the hell' she thought. "Both."

The two of them sat quietly for a while, Tara noticing for the first time that evening that the lights of the Ben Franklin Bridge had been changed to red, white and blue for the upcoming Fourth of July weekend.

After a period of silence it was Kellie who spoke first. "So what are you…gay, straight…bi?"

Tara looked back at Kellie, who was drawing slowly on her newly lit cigarette. She hated having to explain once again that she was just a woman who was open to accepting love, regardless of what form that love came in. "I don't really like labels. I like men mostly but on occasion I've found myself in a relationship with a woman or two."

"Yeah well label or no label…you're bi." Kellie said coarsely.

"If you say so." Tara said trying not to sound offended.

"It's cool Tara" she said dragging on her cigarette deeply, "I check out women all of the time. I once told Covington that I might be attracted to women; it was this model Karina I worked with once, a German blonde..." Kellie paused to drain the rest of her beer. "He told me he wasn't surprised because I was a freak."

'Freak' that word made Tara cringe; she felt a slight tightening of her stomach almost as soon as Kellie said the word. 'Freak' that's what he ex-fiancée Kevin called her when she confided in him that she thought she might be bi. The word hurt her now as much as it did then.

Kevin for his part thought that meant lesbian open season in their bed, he immediately plotted for them to have an ménage a trios, without considering whether Tara was game or not.

He thought that he could bring home any stray woman and Tara would drop everything and have sex with her for his pleasure. It pained her to recall the night he showed up hours late for a romantic dinner with a stripper on his arm grinning like a little boy who'd just found a filthy little alley kitten... "Let me guess, he even suggested bringing a girl home for you as long as he got to watch."

"Wow, how did you know? He says that all of the time."

Tara grimaced, 'cause men think with their dicks' she thought. "Just a lucky guess." She said. 'Just like Kevin', she thought. Kevin was her brilliant beautiful starving architect and Tara fell in love with him almost immediately after they met. Truth be told, she fell in love with his gorgeousness, if she was being honest with herself. Kevin was for lack of a better word, beautiful. Tall with cream colored skin, well chiseled features, a sensuous mouth, dark hair that teasingly curled around his face and eyes that shone with a prism of gold, olive, hazel and warm sienna.

Tara fell quick and hard for Kevin, by her own proposal they were engaged to be married in less than a year. She told herself back then it was fine for them to live off of her salary, after all she had plenty to spare. Kevin, she rationalized just needed his big break, once he was recognized in his field he'd be making a six perhaps seven figure salary.

For five years they lavished off of her income, and Tara crazy about her man, treated him extremely well. He never drove less than a new BMW, she gave him access to her home and her money, in fact anything she owned was his to enjoy. If Tara ate lobster…then Kevin ate lobster.

Eventually he did get his big break, a French architectural firm signed him on to design several sport arenas in South America and one very prominent office building in France. When Kevin became a millionaire in his own right, he broke their engagement and moved to France with his young office assistant, some French girl named Garcelle.

"He asked me about it today as a matter of fact. He wants it to be a threesome."

'Covington the Sleaze' Tara thought. "Yeah, and what did you say to that?"

"I told him that I'm not sure yet, but I'm thinking about it." Kellie replied.

Tara looked back at Kellie and shook her head, 'treats you like shit, and you'd still consider giving him a ménage a trois…incredible' she thought. "You'll figure it out I guess."

The silence ensued again, this time not as comfortable. There were questions floating in the air and it was just of matter of time before they would land on Kellie's lips. Tara could almost hear the words forming in Kellie's mind and she shifted about in her seat. Even in the darkness she could see Kellie's eyes sparkling with interest. "Sooo, Tara…when was the last time, uh, you know?"

"What?" Tara said finishing off her bottle.

"Been with a woman." Kellie said, the words rushing from her mouth.

Tara got up from her chair and walked back into her kitchen, retrieving another Corona Light for herself and one for Kellie from her refrigerator, Kellie followed closely on her heels. Sighing deeply she said, "Jada was my last girlfriend."

"Your old roommate?" Kellie said a little louder than necessary, her brows rising as if a light just came on in her head. Jada was a struggling model like herself. Recently she moved to Miami with her new boyfriend and agent Marco. "Oh." escaped her mouth as she realized that Jada actually left Tara for a guy.

"Yup." Tara said taking a bigger swig than before.

"Wow, I didn't realize."

"It's fine, we're still friends." Tara lied.

'So Tara's into models huh?' she thought. Kellie's back automatically arched sensuously as she leaned across the kitchen counter towards Tara. "You've got good taste Tara." Kellie said, the tone of her voice softening. "Jada was really pretty, I hear she gets a lot of work down in Miami."

"Yeah, she's a cutie." Tara said not wanting to remember the satiny bronze of Jada's skin, the pout of her full lips, the sexy command of her walk.

"Mmm hmm, she is…" Two things were crystal clear to Kellie, one her richer wealthier friend was into sexy model type women; she just happened to be that type of chick. And two no one had replaced Jada in Tara's life, at least not yet; if they had they'd be here right now. Licking her lips making them moist, she leaned in even further whispering sensually, "Mmm hmm, really good taste." Not missing a beat Kellie dove in with, "so tell me Tara…do you find me attractive?"

Tara gave Kellie a full once over. Long legs and a tight body, Kellie had to be at least five nine, five ten perhaps. Her suntanned skin was kissed from head to toe with freckles. Her face was adorned with natural green doe like eyes and a full, pouty pink mouth that made her appear as if she was always puckering up for a kiss. Her hair a wiry mess of reddish brown waves made Kellie the oddest combination of black and Irish that she'd ever seen. Did she find this strange girl attractive? 'Hell yes!' her mind screamed out to her, but she decided not to let Kellie know that, at least not right away. "I dunno, I've never thought about it." She said walking away into her living room.

"That's funny, because I checked you out the moment I saw you." Kellie replied just steps behind Tara. Which was somewhat true, she'd always admired Tara's style. Tara was more handsome than pretty, with high cheekbones, almond shaped eyes, a fine nose and satiny slash of a mouth. Kellie loved the smooth ebony of Tara's athletic frame, years of running kept her tone and shapely, and her short, spiky hairstyle served to make her look sassy and serious all at once.

"Oh really…" 'Cute' Tara thought; Kellie was actually coming on to her. "That's interesting." Kellie's cell phone rang; Tara could tell by the Anthony Hamilton ring tone that it was Kellie's boyfriend Covington calling.

Kellie without even thinking about it silenced her phone then turned it off. 'Got new fish to fry' she thought. Kellie turned to face Tara and asked, "so what's it like."

"What's what like?" 'This girl didn't play', Tara thought noticing the change in Kellie's voice, eyeing the not so subtle vibe of her body language.

"Being with a woman." She said. Kellie was now lying back in Tara's leather sofa, her arms behind her head, one leg dangling over the side and her green eyes focused on Tara like a cat watching her prey.

"It's umm…" Despite herself she couldn't help but notice Kellie's aroused nipples gently protruding from her thin cotton shirt. Tara exhaled a long sigh. Her cool demeanor slightly rattled by the sight of Kellie licking the lips of her full pink mouth. 'Damn' she thought, once again she wished she wasn't so susceptible to this particular weakness. Pretty women, just like pretty men always got the best of her.

Clearing her throat she continued "it's beautiful…when two women truly dig each other, it's really good."

"So how do you know if a woman really digs you?" Kellie said barely above a whisper her hand resting precariously between her thighs.

Tara smiled to herself; she knew she shouldn't let this happen. First and foremost by her own admission Kellie was by nature an opportunist, a gold digger and secondly there was that boyfriend to consider; Covington wouldn't take the news of her pushing up on his girlfriend lying down. Third and most importantly was her public persona; she and Jada had an understanding. When their relationship ended, as painful as it was for her at least Jada went quietly with her new man…no public, no press. With Kellie she wasn't so sure. This girl was at times as flaky as she was calculating. Tara bit her lip, wishing to hell it wasn't after midnight, wishing she wasn't already entranced by Kellie's sensual mood.

The more her mind tried to talk her out of it, the more it didn't matter. All that seemed to matter right now was the rhythmic motion of Kellie's fingers slowly and insistently moving against the thin fabric of her cotton shorts. All she could think of was replacing them with her own fingers or perhaps her mouth or perhaps both.

"You know when just looking at you makes her touch herself."

"Then why aren't you…touching yourself?" Kellie said with a wicked smile on her face.

"I'd rather let you do it." 'Damn' she thought 'no turning back now'.

Kellie moved so quickly from her seat on the sofa to Tara's chaise that Tara barely saw her move. All she saw was a blur as Kellie climbed atop of her instantly locking her in an embrace. Facing each other the two shared their first kiss; from the moment their lips touched Tara's adrenaline coursed through her body like electric.

A flood of sensations filled her as they slowly and deliberately tasted each other's mouths. 'Trouble' Tara thought. This felt better than she realized it would. It hadn't been that long since her lips locked together with a beautiful woman, or a man for that matter, but she never remembered it feeling like this. Tara let her fingers slip inside Kellie's thick hair as she brought their mouths closer together. Together they were swept up in their long, languid, deliberate, passionate kiss.

When they at last separated, Kellie stood up and was completely undressed in seconds, Tara following suit not long after. Tara then laid Kellie back against the chaise and crawled slowly between her legs. It thrilled Tara to discover Kellie's freckles covered every inch of her body, even the smoothly shaved triangle between her legs. With much restraint, Tara took her time as she explored every crevice of Kellie's body with her tongue reveling in her taste and the sound of Kellie's squeals of delight.

When Kellie's voice dropped an octave and she began moaning Tara's name. Tara felt another surge of power course through her. Kellie bucked madly against Tara's tongue, squeezing her thighs holding Tara's head in place. When Kellie was ready to climax, Tara climbed atop of her, sliding two fingers inside of her. Tara kept her gaze focused intently on Kellie's eyes wanting to witness their intensity when she came all over Tara's fingers. Tara continued to manipulate Kellie's body with her hands until she screamed and trembled in pleasure.

When it was her turn, Tara discovered that Kellie was a quick learner, eager to return the favor bringing some tricks of her own to the equation, tempting Tara with pain as well as pleasure as she teased and pleased her. Kellie's hunger was almost surprising to Tara, as she worked passionately with her fingers and mouth as if she had something to prove. Tara thought as Kellie took control.

As the room had become full of their heat and the sounds of their breathing echoed through the apartment Tara felt herself cresting, greedily drawing Kellie's mouth against her locking her fingers in her hair. Tara was almost embarrassed by her loud cry when she came hard against Kellie's face. Kellie's hunger continued long after Tara laid exhausted continuing to taste her until Tara begged her to stop.

After several moments of enjoying the cool breeze drifting off the Delaware through the balcony door Kellie decided to take Tara up on her offer to join her in the Jacuzzi. It was no surprise to either of them that the pressure of the pulsating water had them once again aroused and pleasing each other.

Tara guided Kellie onto the edge of the tub giving her great access to Kellie's treasure. Tara tasted and sucked on her younger friend until Kellie climaxed for a second time. When her trembling ceased, she joined Tara again in the tub so that Tara could show her how to get more pleasure from the water jets as they cascaded across her swollen clit.

Kellie then spread Tara's legs apart and went beneath the water. Displaying her talent for holding her breath, she stayed underwater long enough to bring Tara close to her second orgasm. Coming up for air, Kellie finished Tara off with her fingers and thumb until Tara shuddered another orgasm.

Afterwards they sat in the water gently kissing and massaging each other as they talked. "Wow." Kellie uttered her voice soft and raspy, cuddling up closely to Tara.

"Your first time?" Kellie seemed to know exactly what she was doing.

"Not unless you count making out with your best friend at your thirteenth birthday slumber party." Kellie said giggling.

"No, we won't count that." Tara laughed, climbing out the tub.

"Then you're my first girl on girl experience." Kellie replied giddily, right behind her noticing for the first time how round Tara's ass was; reaching out she gave it a nice squeeze.

Surprised Tara looked back at Kellie and smiled, there was still passion stirring in Kellie's eyes, "not done yet huh?"

Kellie looked Tara's naked body over greedily and replied, "nope…not done yet."

Without drying off, Tara took Kellie by the hand and led her down the hall to her bedroom, she knew what Kellie needed and couldn't wait to give it to her. In the bedroom, Tara directed Kellie to lie down on her bed then reached in her drawer and pulled out a strap on dildo. Once she was harnessed up she slid a condom on it and with a little lubricant entered Kellie.

Kellie for her part lost control, she moved against the dildo like a wild animal. 'Just like Jada' Tara thought as she stroked her hips athletically towards Kellie's writhing body. Grabbing her by the hips Tara moved more and more forcefully into her, then having Kellie turn over face down, took her doggie style rougher than she had before.

Tara watched herself in her mirror, her body moved like Kevin's used to back when they were still together. Keeping her back straight, as she rolled her hips forward just as she'd learned from watching him. This drove Jada crazy, left her begging and begging for more, just like Kellie was doing right now.

Kellie's whole body was covered in sweat as she cursed under her breath, shocked that she could get this kind of sex from a woman. Sex with Covington was never this good, in fact it had never been this good with any man she'd ever been with. When Tara placed a lubricated finger inside her ass and began stroking it in and out gently, Kellie thought she would lose her mind. Tara learned this from Kevin too.

Kellie was unfamiliar with this sensation, but loving it. Soon, very soon a satisfied groan drew its way from Kellie's mouth as she came yet a third time that evening, this time looking completely exhausted. Collapsing on the bed Kellie said nothing; she just clung to Tara tightly then in minutes was soundly off to sleep.

Lying in the bed next to sleeping Kellie, Tara checked her clock for the time. It was already close to four thirty am, 'almost morning' she thought. A lot had happened since Kellie arrived at midnight but Tara wasn't quite convinced that all of it was a good.

But it was good to have a warm body next to her in her bed again, she of course would have preferred it to be Kevin before he hurt her so many years ago or Jada whose presence was so recent, Tara still thought she smelled her perfume around the apartment. But it wasn't it, was this pretty freckled woman with the red hair who had 'more than a little bit of shit going on with her', Tara thought. Too tired to give it much more thought, she wrapped her arms around Kellie and fell off to sleep as well.

Tara awoke hours later to the smell of food cooking, eggs. Glancing at the clock she realized it was after ten am; she'd been asleep for hours. It was cool though since Sunday was the only morning in which her show didn't air live, she recorded segments for this mornings run yesterday before she left the station. For a moment she thought 'Jada must be making breakfast,' then she remembered Jada was gone. As the events from the night before cleared her groggy mind she realized who was in the kitchen preparing food. It was Kellie.

Tara quickly cleaned herself up in the bathroom, brushing her teeth and smoothing down her ruined hairdo. Slipping on a tee and shorts, she headed out of her bedroom to talk with Kellie. She'd made up her mind to tell Kellie that last night hadn't been such a good idea. After all, she was just coming off of her break up with Jada and Kellie had her situation with Covington to deal with. For her, at least last night served only to temporarily take away some of the loneliness.

She rehearsed in her head over and over again exactly what she would say. She'll tell her that she wanted to remain friends but what happened between them really shouldn't happen again. Tara just hoped Kellie would be mature about it the last thing she wanted was for the public to get a whiff of their one night stand. She was all ready to jump into her spiel when on her way to the kitchen; she noticed the row of at least seven pieces of Louis Vuitton luggage in her foyer. She absently wondered how much the luggage and in the contents inside set old Covington back. Trouble.

"Kel?" Tara said walking into the kitchen her hand pointing towards the luggage at the door with a bewildered look on her face. Kellie was standing in the kitchen, dressed in a casual strapless top, denim mini skirt and flip flops, wearing Tara's apron, her hair freshly washed and pulled back into a ponytail. Smiling, she placed in front of Tara on the marble breakfast bar a vegetable omelet and a tall raspberry mimosa.

"I thought about what you said Tara," Kellie said her words rushing out of her mouth while her hands steadily worked about the kitchen, "and you're right, I've stayed with Covington for all of the wrong reasons. While you were sleep I took the elevator down to his place and told him so."

His place "You did what?"

"Yup, I told him, I was tired of us fighting all of the time and that I needed to move on." Kellie said, busily placing a napkin and silverware next to Tara's plate. Reaching into the refrigerator Kellie pulled out a melon salad and placed it next to the mimosa. "And you know what he said…he said I was a simpleton who wouldn't last a minute without him, do you believe that?" Kellie bit down on her lip trying to slow down her talking. She felt like she was on a very important job interview and her goal was to nail the position; she had to sell herself, sell Tara a situation, hoping upon hope that she hadn't played herself.

Who'd a thought rich miss Tara was into females. If she'd known that she wouldn't have come here bitching about Covington. Hell, not only did Tara have a bigger and nicer place than Covington, but she had more money and fucked better too! Thinking back to the night before, she remembered how into her Tara was, so she couldn't see how she could lose.

"All of that happened this morning?" Tara said incredulously looking down at the omelet in front of her, it looked delicious. She thought about the bags in the foyer, how the hell she slept through all this activity was beyond her.

"Yup Covington said, I was just another dizzy model and I'd be back before the week was out." He said a lot more than that, he also called her a conniving, gold digging, slut that he should have left at the bus stop in Center City where he found her, but Kellie decided to leave that part out.

'Model maybe, dizzy no; this chick knows exactly what she's doing' Tara thought. "And what did you say to that?" Despite herself she'd began eating the omelet, it tasted as good as it looked.

"I told him he was wrong, that I was getting good work, my career was taking off. I told him I'd be able to afford my own place real soon."

"What did you tell him you were going to do in the meantime?" Tara asked already knowing the answer.

"Well...I told him if I had to I would move back with my mom and my aunts in Santa Barbara or... see if I could room with you until I got on my feet." Kellie gushed out eyeing Tara's response to this searching her face trying to read her.

'Slick chick...real slick' Tara thought. "Room with me huh?"

"I mean I would take any room you gave me, and of course I would pay you rent..." Kellie tried her best to say this with a straight face.

'Yeah I know' Tara thought, 'you put down one months rent and two months security last night.' "Any room?" Tara asked, looking at Kellie's freckles; wishing once again that pretty girls weren't her weakness.

Picking up Tara's fork Kellie put a nice size bite of the omelet in her mouth, chewing slowly, deliberately, not replying until she swallowed her bite. "That is, unless you'd like me to stay in your room, with you."

Tara's eyebrows raised, she thought she was the one with the prepared speech; this girl was head and shoulders above her. "That's a lot of stuff to fit in my room." Tara said nodding towards the foyer.

"Oh...I mean I could keep my stuff in another room, maybe in Jada's old room. But I'd be happy to spend as many nights as you wanted in your room. Kellie said picking up a piece of honeydew and biting in, letting the juices run down her chin.

"What if I said no?" Tara said testing her.

'You won't' Kelly thought, "Then I be on a plane to California today, and hopefully I'd get some work out there. I've been doing so good here on the east coast, but…" Kellie said trying her best to sound pitiful.

Tara sighed, Kevin, Jada, and now Kellie. They all had a hustle; each of them wanted something from her…namely her money. 'One day' she hoped to find a partner, someone who wanted her for her, there had to be someone out there.

But in the meantime there was this. She looked Kellie over again, sizing her up; did she want to take on the role of Sugar Momma again? Tara weighed the pros and cons; if nothing else the company and the sex would be welcome. 'It could be worse' she thought; taking another bite of her food thinking again how delicious the omelet was; 'she could be a gold digger who couldn't cook'. "That's not necessary," she said seeing the anticipation in Kellie's eyes, "you're welcome to stay."

"Oh thank you!" Kelly gushed wrapping her arms around Tara, kissing her cheek.

Tara finished up her breakfast still wondering what she'd gotten herself into, while Kellie ran out to the foyer to get her bags.

As she unpacked in her new bedroom, Kellie sighed deeply a sigh of relief. She glanced around the bedroom that she knew would be used only to store her clothes; she would be sleeping in the master bedroom, where she belonged. Then she walked to the window taking in the magnificent view from twenty-nine flights above the ground and smiled to herself, satisfied. There was something else her mother always said 'If your gonna make a move, then make sure the move is up!' She couldn't get any further up than the penthouse.

Kellie turned and sashayed back to her unpacking twisting her hips as she moved to the sound of her theme song playing for her over and over again in her head. *Get down girl, go 'head get down.*

The Candy Man

Lailah was stressed so stressed her girlfriend Maritza didn't even recognize her voice when she phoned in to call out for the day. "Ritz, do me a favor girl...tell Carol I won't be in today."

"Bet you caught that bug that's going around."

"Naw, it's more mental than physical."

"You alright Lah'?"

"Yeah, I'll be alright...I guess." Lailah said not sounding sure at all.

"You feel like talking about it?" Marissa asked.

Lailah didn't know where to start, her mind was wound so tight, and she was sure if she started talking right now, she'd probably snap. "No, not yet."

"What are your gonna do with your day?" Marissa asked.

"Just hang around here I guess. Maybe get some more rest."

Maritza was silent for a, moment on the phone line, and then said, "Listen, when was the last time you pampered yourself, like got your hair done."

"Girl with my budget, and you know all that talk about layoffs, I don't have any extra money..."

"Nevertheless you have to take out some time for yourself."

"Right now, a hairstyle is the last thing on my mind."

"It should be the first." Maritza replied. "Take care of you, and the rest of your problems; that's including that no good boyfriend of yours and this damn job; will take care of themselves."

Lailah tried to chuckle through the tension headache that was building in her head. Maritza knew exactly what was bothering her without Lailah having to say a word. "I hear you girl."

"No sense in looking as raggedy as you feel. Everything doesn't have to go to pot…you know what I mean?"

"That makes sense."

"Look I want you to do something today, and don't worry this one, is on me." Maritza began.

"Oh, Ritz you don't have to." Lailah objected.

"Girl, shut up. I know a potential burnout when I see one. You need intervention. Now I want you to go see my stylist Candy, trust me you'll walk out there looking and feeling a lot better. Candy is a good listener."

"Ritz, I'm not about to sit in some salon chair and blab all my business in front of a shop full of women." Lailah argued.

"What shop full? Candy does hair right at home, in a private salon in the basement. Look I owe you for babysitting the twins, let me be the good friend you are to me, and do this for you."

Lailah sighed, she knew Maritza wasn't going to let up, and getting her hair done on a hooky day beat sitting around wallowing in her drama called life any day. "Ok."

"That a girl! I'll call Candy to see what time you can get fit in and then call you back with an appointment time."

"Ok, and thanks Ritz." Lailah said truly grateful to have such a caring friend.

Lailah pulled herself up from the bed, slowly now that her headache was full blown. Walked to the bathroom, opened the medicine cabinet and popped two extra strength Motrin's in her mouth following it with two handfuls of sink water.

Lailah considered her reflection in the mirror. She couldn't even tell if she was still attractive or not, her olive complexion looked pasty and dull. Her dark brown eyes looked tired, all puffy underneath and the beginning of wrinkles creasing at the corners.

Her hair was an over grown mess of auburn ends and tightly wound dark roots, there were even a few grays beginning to peek out at her temples. "Get it together girl, you're only thirty one." Lailah said out loud to herself.

As she stood under a steaming shower she knew what was bothering her…practically everything. She'd known for some time that her boyfriend of six years was up to no good, but when a girl no more than sixteen showed up at her door seven months pregnant claiming Marcus to be the father, Lailah felt like someone hit her with a falling boulder.

Then her manager Carol came in the next day informing them all of an impending layoff, just a week after she made settlement on her house in the Oxford Circle.

From that it fell like dominos, she'd gotten a speeding ticket on her way home last night, climbing out her car she broke the heel of her expensive 9West shoes, once she was in her house, her brother called needing to borrow four hundred dollars that she didn't have to bail his rowdy girlfriend once again from jail, and then her new next door neighbor banged on her door practically cussing her out for "stealing" his parking space. Lailah still wondered how in the hell did someone own a parking space on the street in Philadelphia. It was just icing on the cake when all of the power on the block went out and PECO wasn't sure if it would be back on anytime soon.

Lailah just laid there in the darkness with a glass of Alize' in her hand, trying to will herself to sleep. Turning off the phone so that Marcus couldn't call any more, she decided to let him leave messages to tell her of how ridiculous she was being, how she was acting like a child instead of a full grown woman about the situation.

Standing in the hot shower, she wondered why she let things go on with Marcus for so long, he was lousy in bed yet he still cheated on her each and every chance he got. He was cheap; he'd never so much as brought her a Valentine's Day card, and talk about emotionally unavailable; Marcus rarely showed her or her feelings any real concern.

Drying off, she wondered about her own actions and knew she was to blame. She should have kicked him off sideways a long time ago; maybe she was hoping he'd change. Maybe; she realized; it just felt good to say you had a man. 'Half a man is better than no man at all,' her mother used to say, but this time Momma was wrong. It was hard loving a man who no matter what you did, didn't want to love you back faithfully. The teenager with the bulging belly was the final straw. She was cutting Marcus loose.

Smoothing lotion on her skin, Lailah didn't even notice the fine curve as her back flowed into the round of her ample butt, the way her full breast made her waist look even tinier than it already was, the smooth length of her strong thighs as they sat atop her long flawless legs. No, Marcus and all of his cheating made her forget how truly sexy a woman she was.

As she got dressed she wondered what else Murphy's Law had in store for her. Not only had she just lost her man, but according to Carol, her job as well, and her new house would probably soon follow if she didn't find substantial work real quick. Lailah thought, if these past couple days were any indication of her Karma, she must have done something horrible in her past life to deserve all of this.

Her cell phone rang, she saw that it was coming from work and started not to answer, and then she remembered that Maritza would be calling her back with an appointment time so she caught it on the last ring. "Hello?"

"Hey Lah, just got of the phone with my stylist, you can go right now if you want, Candy is free all morning."

"Thanks girl." Lailah replied than jotted down the Northeast Philly address before grabbing her coat and heading out the door.

It took less than ten minutes for her little Honda to zip her north up the Roosevelt Boulevard to Candy's place in the Greater Northeast section of Philadelphia. Candy's neighborhood was really nice, tall trees, green lawns and manicured bushes framed the air light and split level houses of the tightly developed area.

Arriving at the address, Lailah saw it was the end unit and the entrance to the salon was on the side of the house. She walked up to the door with a neatly painted wooden sign that read "The Candy Shop" swinging above and pressed the doorbell.

A man; a fine man; about six feet tall with a deep brown complexion, copper brown eyes, thick silky eyelashes and brows, a full mouth, neatly trimmed mustache and a head of freshly done braids answered the door.

"Good Morning Pretty Lady, you must be Lailah." He said as the diamond studs in his ears shone in the morning sun.

Lailah stepped in from out of the early autumn breeze, surprised to see such an elegant salon situated in someone's basement. "Yes I am, I have an appointment with Candy this morning." Lailah explained as he took her coat. 'This must be her man…go Candy!' Lailah thought as she walked in past him.

"Yup I know I've been waiting for you." He replied standing over a half a foot above Lailah. Lailah looked confused as the man extended his hand to her. "Candrell

Williams…some people call me 'Rell' but most of my friends like to call me, Candy."

"Oh." Lailah said feeling a warm rush of embarrassment flow to her cheeks. She'd just assumed Candy would be a woman, not this good looking, broad shouldered specimen in front of her.

Lailah looked at his extended large hand, it was twice the size of hers, and she began feeling a little nervous. Maritza should have warned her that Candy was a guy, she thought. Looking down she saw his feet dressed in comfortable leather slide ons, were just as large. Candrell didn't look like any hairdresser she'd ever seen before.

'Mmm, hmm' she thought, 'no wonder Maritza kept her hair appointments faithfully. Then she just as quickly checked herself; a good-looking man like him, with a beautiful hair salon and a name like Candy was probably as into men as she was. With that thought, she let herself relax and smile back. "Nice to meet you Candy." She said returning his handshake.

"Come on in honey…have a seat." Candy set directing her to his chair.

Lailah put her handbag down and let herself settle into the orange leather stylist chair. She looked around the room taking in the décor while Candy busied himself in hanging up her coat for her. The walls were a deep eggplant purple almost black with large ornate oversized gold framed mirrors. From the ceiling hung an ornate chandelier with matching wall sconces around the room.

He had two shampoo sinks, two hood dryers, a powder room, a waiting area that consisted of a large orange sofa, glass coffee table, a purple side chair and what looked to be a changing room with an orange crushed silk curtain for a door.

Besides that, there were two stations. Candy's that was covered with curlers and hair products and another, which looked vacant. Both were made of light birch, stained orange to match the chairs. On the walls were gold framed pictures of who she assumed was Candy's clients, then she was certain they were when she saw a picture of Maritza with her hair all freshly done up in soft, shiny curls.

"You're clients?" Lailah asked.

"I prefer to call 'em my girlfriends, these here are my ladies. I'm much more than just their stylist you know."

"That's sweet." Lailah replied. 'He was probably just as much their girlfriend as well', she thought. Taking a deep breath trying to relax in her chair Lailah began sipping from the cup of herbal tea that Candy offered her.

"So let me take a look at this head of yours beautiful." Candy said running his fingers through her hair. When Lailah jumped at his touched it didn't go unnoticed by him. Candy frowned in concern, "tender headed, Lailah?" he asked.

"No, not really." Lailah responded.

"Mmm, hmm." Candy said as if he understood. Placing his two hands on her shoulders Candy felt her neck and shoulder muscles were pulled tight like a drum. He looked down at her hands, curled in a fist, her thighs squeezed together tightly. "Let me try this." He said massaging his fingers in slow circular motions through her scalp down to her nape.

"That feels kinda nice." Lailah said though still feeling tense.

"Sugar, what's happened to you to make you so stressed, so uptight?"

Lailah thought about it, the last couple of days were just the icing on the cake, things had been going south for quite a while, especially with her relationship. "I wouldn't even know where to start Candy." Lailah answered honestly.

Candy turned her around in her chair and said, "you know something, before I start on that head of yours I'd like to see you relax a little more, what do you think?"

"Umm, I don't know." Lailah answered not knowing what he meant.

"Listen, I don't know if Maritza told you, but I also give massages…good ones. I usually charge sixty dollars for an hour, but you're a special case, by the look of the knots in your shoulders and back, I'd say you need my assistance ASAP. How about letting me remove some of that pressure from you, that way you'll enjoy getting you hair done instead of tensing up into a ball every time I touch you."

"Umm, I don't know." Getting her hair done was one thing, but letting this man rub all over her was another. Lailah didn't know him from Adam.

Candy sensed her apprehension. "Tell you what, give Maritza a call, she can probably better than anyone tell you how good a Candy Man massage will help you feel." Candy excused himself and ran upstairs for a moment while she placed her call.

Lailah still unsure flipped open her phone and dialed her work number, grateful it was Maritza who answered and not Carol. She quickly told her about Candy's offer to help her relax and her own reservations, "Girl, I do not know this man."

"So he offered you a massage huh, he must like you, Candy doesn't do that for everybody."

"So it's a good idea?"

"Let me put it this way, Candy has a way of giving you exactly what you need…when you need it. If he offers you a massage, then momma, that's probably exactly what you need right now."

Lailah regarded Candy as he returned to the shop; perhaps a good massage would help her, who wouldn't welcome a nice rubdown from those strong looking hands. Lailah didn't know what to expect though, she'd never had a professional massage before. "Thanks girl." Lailah said closing her phone after a quick goodbye.

"Well?" Candy asked refreshing her tea.

"Ritz thought it was a great idea." Lailah said smiling.

"I'm pretty sure she did, she's gotten some of my best sessions."

"Ok," Lailah said getting excited, "what do I need to do?"

"Behind that curtain is my massage room, go in, get undressed and make yourself comfortable on the table."

"Undressed!?"

"Don't worry there is sheet and towel in there to keep you covered." Then he added, "Pick out something you like to hear while you're getting your massage, I have cds' on a shelf in there."

"Thanks, Candy." Lailah said beginning to feel a little better already. If this felt as great as she hoped it would maybe she would try to fit a massage into her budget from time to time. That was, once she found a new job.

Pulling back the curtain, Lailah was surprised by what she saw. The little room was a lot larger than she thought it would be. The room was all white with Asian Jade and cherry wood accents; she noticed the inside of the curtain was of jade colored silk.

In the center was a table with a donut shaped pillow at the end of it. The middle of the table and some type of Chinese lettering on it as did a screen that she assumed she was to change her clothes behind. There was a small sound system, cds, towels, candles, and rows of oils and lotions in pretty bottles on one wall on a set of randomly placed cherry wood shelves. In one corner was a jade green satin slipper chair and a small table to place her things, in a diagonal corner was a row of mini bonsai trees and more jade figurines.

Lailah undressed, wrapped herself in a towel and went to the rows of cds. She thought she'd find a selection of music there, but instead there was a row of different kinds of relaxation cds.

She perused through the titles wondering which one would help lift her spirits. There was, 'Mystic Jungle', 'Tropical Waterfall', 'Exotic Ocean', 'Birds and Animals' (that one sounded too weird). Then she came upon 'Tranquil Rain', and thought 'perfect'.

"Can I come in?" She heard Candy say as she picked her selection off the shelf.

"Yup, I'm ready." Lailah said handing Candy the cd as he pulled back the curtain.

"Mmm, good one." He said then directed her to lie on the table face down. Candy discreetly removed her towel as he covered her body with a white cotton sheet, and then went about the task of lighting candles and incense and starting up the cd she chose.

Lailah laid there as the room filled with the sound of gently pouring rain, surprised at how the sound instantly transported her to being a little girl sitting on her grandparents' porch down south. She remember sitting on her grandmother's rocking chair sipping lemonade watching as the summer rain poured down gently in the afternoon. 'Nice' she thought, mental pictures like these hadn't come to mind like that for her in years.

Candy pulled the sheet down, exposing Lailah's back. As his warm hand made contact with her skin the room filled with fragrance; it was a mixture of the incense and the fresh eucalyptus and berry scented oil he was massaging into her skin.

Candy started at the center of her back, moving his thumbs and fingers in outward motions away from her spine; taking with them a line of tension she didn't realize was there.

His hands worked upward, beneath her shoulder blades, then over. Candy patiently took as much time with her arms hands and fingers as he did with her shoulders and neck.

Lailah could feel the blood circulating freer through the top half of her body as she listened to the sounds of torrential rain and wind wafting through the air.

Candy returned to her spine, gently moving the negative tension up and outward through her arms and out through her fingertips.

Candy spoke very little; he'd just give her one-word phrases to help her enjoy the process even more. "Breath", "relax", "enjoy", "release", he'd say to her in a deep comforting tone as her massaged more of the deliciously scented oil into her body.

He instructed her to lift her arms above her head as he smoothed his palms down the length of her sides, once again, up and out towards her arms and fingertips.

Candy now moved his hands in little chopping motions up and down the length of her back, stopping only to massage little circles beneath her lungs and at her kidneys, encouraging her to breathe deeply as he did.

Covering her back and arms again with the sheet to keep them warm, Candy lifted the bottom of the sheet, exposing her thighs, legs and feet. With a little more pressure than before he began to kneed the back of her thighs, sliding his strong hands up, down, around and between, releasing pressure from her ham strings, then her calves, ankles, heels, feet and toes.

Using his forearms, Candy slid his arms in alternate motions completely down the length of both of her legs, stopping at her calves.

Moving back upwards again, his hands continued to move this time past the sheet onto her butt cheeks, moving her roundness around in his palms. When Candy took the side of her left cheek and moved it up and over the bone with his left fist and massaged his right fist gently into the firm flesh there, Lailah suddenly felt a sensation that was a little more than tense muscles relaxing. His slow deliberate movement of her ass was suddenly turning her on.

"Mmm", she heard herself moan out loud as he moved on to the right cheek raising the muscle high with one closed fist and kneading it deeply with the other.

"Like that?" Candy asked her, his strong hands still manipulating her glutes like they were no more than putty.

"Mmm Hmm", was her reply as she continued to rest her head on the comfortable donut. With her eyes closed enjoying the sensation she didn't notice the rise in Candy's loose fitting pants as he continued her massage.

Candy opened his hands and massaged her butt with his open palms, adding more of the oil to his hands. The slippery oil caused his thumbs to slip precariously close to Lailah's anus, causing her to jump a little.

"You ok?" Candy asked withdrawing his hands.

"Um...I'm fine." Lailah said, embarrassed as a surge of moisture coursed between her legs. Candy's massage was making her incredibly horny, she wasn't sure if it was normal to feel that way or not. "I just have to pee."

"Oh ok, that's cool, " Candy said remembering she'd had two cups of herbal tea. "I was just about to ask you to turn around so I guess this is a good breaking point." Candy said turning his head as she covered herself with the towel. "Would you mind if I put on a different cd?"

"No that's fine." She said padding off to the powder room. Lailah quickly went to the bathroom, taking a moment to freshen herself up, hoping Candy didn't notice her arousal.

Returning to the massage room, Candy stood there awaiting her, the soft sounds of chimes and quiet drums playing now. He'd removed the donut from the table and raised a length at the foot to make it longer.

She realized for the first time since she'd gotten to the Candy Shop that she hadn't thought about Marcus, work or anything else that had her stressed out earlier.

"Ready to go?" Candy asked her, smiling.

"Yup," she answered, climbing back on the table, this time reclining on her back. Looking up at Candy as he once again discretely replaced her towel with the sheet all without exposing her; she decided to ask him what was on her mind.

"Candy is it normal for…I mean does any of your other client get…?" Lailah was having trouble putting her question into words.

"Turned on by their massage?" Candy said standing over her looking into her eyes.

"Well, yeah…I guess I kinda did." Lailah said feeling the heat rise in her face from embarrassment.

"Given the right kind of stimulation, the body releases what it needs to release to bring it back to balance. It's not uncommon if your body needs sexual release to be turned on by a massage."

"Oh." Lailah responded, grateful that his answer sounded more scientific than she expected.

"You know Lailah, this is your massage, your hour. Feel free to take from it what you want, don't be embarrassed to let yourself go if you want to."

Lailah relaxed again at his words, and enjoyed the feel of him massaging her temples, forehead, cheeks and chin. Her eyes once again closed, Lailah listened as the sound of the chimes danced in her ears, the soft drum matching the sound of her breathing deeply.

Candy moved his fingers down to her neck, chest and arms. He once again massaged her arms, down to the fingertips and back again. Leaning over her head, his hands were now just above her breast. "Ok, beautiful" he began, "I can give you a complete massage or you can tell me if you want me to skip an area, ok."

"Ok." Lailah said as he waited for her permission to lower the sheet. "You can go ahead." Lailah responded, anticipating the feel of his hands on the rest of her.

With that, Candy lowered the sheet to just below her belly and began massaging the oil in his open palm all around her navel. His hands moved deftly, the heels of his palms gently moving her relaxed belly back and forth.

"Mmm, this is great Candy," Lailah said her eyes still watching him intently as he moved his hands up and down her sides, turning inward toward her navel each time.

Then his hands slid up above her breast again and rested there for a moment, waiting for her cue to go ahead.

"It's okay." Lailah said. First he massaged under her armpits and her sides, telling her to breath in and out as he stimulated her lungs and spleen. As soon as his fingers touched the swell of her breast, Lailah's nipples became erect and her breath deepened. Once again she felt wetness begin to seep between her legs.

She was on fire as his fingers insistently circled first the fullness of her breast then the dark areola surrounding her nipples. By the time his fingers were gently rubbing her nipples, Lailah had slipped her right hand between her legs. She wanted so badly to touch herself, but she hesitated.

"Go ahead, like I said, this for you." Candy urged her.

And she did, slowly at first; a little embarrassed. Then her fingers picked up speed, her circling motion began matching the tempo of Candy's hands and the soft drums still playing.

"Mmm", she uttered looking up into Candy's eyes, now lowered almost covered by his long dark eyelashes.

"That's right gorgeous, let it go", he encouraged her, "let it all go".

Lailah continued to follow the tempo of the drums as she slid her fingers in and out making them slick with wetness. She felt her clitoris become harder and harder as she flicked her fingertip across, then retuned to dipping her fingers deep inside. Slowly at first her hips raised off the table to meet the strokes of her fingers, then faster and harder as her need increased. "Oh, Candy!" She said beginning to feel herself close to cumming.

Candy brought his face down close to her and whispered in her ear, "let it out Lailah, give it to Candy, give it to me baby."

The sensuous sound of Candy's voice, and his delicious male scent was too much for her. Lailah felt the tremors first in her legs and in her belly, and then it spread rapidly throughout her entire body. Her hand became covered with wetness as she came hard all over her fingers, one pulsating wave after another. What started as a low moan turned into a roaring cry with each multiple orgasm. "YES!" she cried, "YES, CANDY YES!" she screamed as her hips bucked forward and the strongest of the waves overtook her.

Once her trembling stopped and Lailah laid there exhausted, Candy walked around to the side of the table, covered her top half with the sheet again, then reached down and gave her an earnest hug. "That's what you needed baby, to let go," he said, then after a warm kiss on her cheek proceeded to complete her massage; though her thighs, legs, feet and toes were already completely relaxed. He gently let his fingers knead her muscles with a little more of the oil as she fought to compose herself.

"Thank you Candy," she said finally.

"No, thank you." Candy said smiling, putting the finishing touches on her toes. "Just think, I was gonna hang out and watch soaps all day."

"You don't have any other appointments today?" Lailah asked, sitting up on the side of the table still wrapped in her towel, while watching Candy blow out the candles.

"Nope, I decided to take a day off, had a hectic weekend." He answered over his shoulder.

"Oh, I'm sorry Candy." Lailah said feeling guilty for invading his day.

"I'm not." Candy replied turning to face her.

That was the first time Lailah noticed how aroused Candy was, there was an impressive tent in his drawstring pants, and from the look in his eyes he was as turned on has she'd been. 'Guess that mean's he does like women', Lailah thought to herself, feeling her own passion rising up again. "You're not?" she asked her voice dropping again.

"Nope", Candy said standing in front of her open legs, biting down on his lip, wetting it with his tongue. "Not at all."

Lailah noticed the height of his crotch was at a perfect angle if he wanted to slide himself into her. He stood perfectly still, taking in the body he'd just become well acquainted with, the hunger apparent in his eyes. She realized, that Candy wasn't going to make a move unless she encouraged it and she admired his restraint. He'd patiently taken care of her; she thought, without asking for anything in return. Not even his usual sixty-dollar fee.

She wanted to do something for him now, show her appreciation for how good he'd just been to her. Lailah wanted him to feel as good as she was feeling right now; relaxed, satisfied, attended to. That, and the fact that she was dying to find out how it would feel to have all of what was rising in his pants inside of her. Lailah in all her life had never seen a bulge so long and thick.

Lailah reached her hands up and touched his face with her hands, Candy responded by kissing the palm of each of her hands. Reaching her hands around to the back of his head she locked her fingers tightly behind his braids and drew his face in for a kiss.

Their lips touched gently at first, then with more passion as his mouth opened to taste hers. Lailah relaxed as he explored the inside of her mouth, wrapping his large hands tightly around her waist.

Letting her towel fall, she guided Candy's mouth to her still sensitive nipples and moaned as he sucked and kissed first her right then her left. "Candy…I want you."

Candy said nothing as he slid his shirt over his head and let his cotton pants fall to the floor.

Lailah stopped a moment to take in his physique, impressed with his lean strong arms, chiseled upper body, tight stomach and powerful legs. She let her fingers trace the block letters of his tattoo that read 'Candy Man' over his right pectoral.

Then her hands traveled down his chest and stomach, loving the feel of his smooth shaved skin and the steel hard muscle underneath.

When her hands reached his hardness, she was surprised and excited to see she needed two hands to grip him.

Candy let out a deep moan as she began stroking him with her hands. Reaching behind himself, he picked up a different bottle of oil and squeezed a little into Lailah's open palms. Lailah took in the sandalwood scent as she stroked his length. The oil seemed to warm beneath her touch as she continued to stroke him.

"You like that?" Lailah asked returning his question from earlier.

"Yeah, but I'd like this even more." Candy said sliding a finger in her wetness.

Lailah' s thighs opened instantly at his touch. The scent of her arousal filling both of their noses, fueling Candy's desire for him even more. "Then take it", she said.

"Be right back." Candy said, exiting the booth. Lailah watched him, amused at his long erection as it bobbed as he walked. Candy returned not moments later with two foiled packaged condoms in his hand.

Lailah took one package and tore it open with her teeth, and with one smooth movement, slid the condom on for him and secured it in place.

Candy drew Lailah's hips to him, wrapping her legs around his waist. Entering her, he was met with some resistance from her tightness, then her body opened up welcoming half of him inside.

Lailah reached underneath grabbing his ass, pulling him in deeper, then when she was satisfied she'd fit as much of his length inside that would fit, she relaxed letting go allowing her body to recline across the massage table with her head hanging over the other side.

Candy laid one of his hands against Lailah's smooth mound letting his thumb tease her clit as he bounced her body back and forth against her, straining to fill her up even more. His other hand extending pinching and toying with the nipple of her bouncing left breast.

Lailah lifted her head to see Candy intently watching himself stroke in and out of her. The intense look of concentration in his eyes turning her on even more. When their eyes met, Lailah thought she would melt right there in his gaze.

Neither of them spoke as lifted her hips to match his stroke; the room was silent except for the sound of their breath and Candy's occasional moan. Even the cd that was playing with its chimes and soft drums came to a silent end.

Candy reached down and lifted Lailah up off the table, supporting her whole weight as his hips continued to stroke forward into her.

Lailah wrapped her arms around his neck kissing his face and neck as her body finally opened to take all of him.

Candy feverishly stroked her, her round ass bouncing against his thighs making a loud smacking sound with each stroke.

Close to cumming, Candy leaned against the wall of the small room, neither caring as a couple of bottles of oil tumbled down to the floor. Candy slid himself down lower, his knees bent, feeling every ounce of Lailah weight as he plunged her down on him. As he came he held her steady, letting her feel the thrust as each stream pumped from him like a geyser.

Lailah thought he was satisfied until he turned her around laying her face down on the massage table, her legs spread, her feet flat on the floor. Sliding the second condom on himself, her took her from behind, making her thighs and knees week as he plowed himself into her.

The harder he stroked her, the louder Lailah cried and moaned from the pleasure. By the time he came the second time, she joined him just moments before she felt him soften inside her.

Candy left the room a second time, this time returning with a cloth, towel and soap for her to freshen herself up with.

This time as Lailah sat in his stylist chair, they both talked and laughed easily. Candy applied a relaxer to her tangles, and then after a shampoo, rinse and condition added a temporary color to hide her darkened roots and few scattered gray hairs.

Lailah told Candy all about Marcus, and like a good friend he listened, gave some advice and then made a joke to alleviate the seriousness. She talked about her job, her fears about her new house, her brother's girlfriend, and her neighbors…everything that previously had her upset.

By the time her hair was smoothly cut, curled and styled, Lailah was feeling ten times happier and calmer. Her problems were still there, but now she felt she could deal with them…one problem at a time.

When Candy handed her a mirror to check out her reflection, she was surprised to see her old self, smiling back at her.

Checking her clock, she'd been at Candy's for over three hours. A lot had happened in that time to make her feel happier, fresher, renewed. She knew she had Candy to thank for that.

Just a little after noon, Candy was walking Lailah to the door, both of them laughing. When he opened the door for her to leave their eyes connected once more.

Candy instinctively bent down to kiss Lailah on the lips and when he did, desire stirred in his belly for her once more.

Dropping her handbag, their lips still locked, Lailah let him lead her to the orange sofa in his waiting area, but resisted a little when he tried to lay her on her back. "But Candy, what about my hair?"

As he continued kissing her, pulling her arms free of her coat he whispered in her ear, "don't worry baby…the Candy Man can fix it."

Hood Boy

"Meeka, aren't you tired of slumming?" Jason asked me, as I got dressed, getting ready to meet my girls in the old neighborhood.

"It wasn't a slum when you were growing up there, was it?" I asked him. I was tired of Jason putting down our old hood.

"That was different, things have changed since then." He said reclining in our four post bed flicking through cable channels with his remote control.

"So things have changed, a lot of the same people are still there." I said touching up my lip-gloss in the mirror.

"Yeah, I know they're there and I left them there…for a reason." Jason said sounding his usual haughty self.

"And what is that?" I asked.

"They're broke and I'm not." Jason answered laughing, but to me sounding pitifully cocky.

"I don't find that funny Jason." I said seriously.

He went on, "Man I can't stop for gas up there without somebody trying sell me something."

I understood what he was saying, about all the guys selling bootleg movies and DVD's, body oils even clothes and sneakers out of a duffle bag, but they were just trying to make a hustle. "Yeah well," I said, "not everyone had your opportunities Jason. At least they're out there trying to make a dollar… it's not like they tried to take anything from you."

"That's alright, I'll leave them right where they are." He said smugly still flipping channels.

"One day, you'll realize Jason, money don't make you better than other people." I said smacking my lips together in the mirror admiring my reflection. "I know one thing, I liked you a whole lot better before you had it."

"So what's wrong with me now?" Jason asked lying there in silk pajamas bottoms and no shirt.

"Who you were back then was exciting, fun, a little rough… guess I miss that." Jason used to be a young thug, a street corner hustler, but with the help of his mother's pastor and a really great teacher got his life on track…literally.

They got him interested in running, and he was good too, so good his running quickly pulled him away from the corner, away from the streets.

That changed his life, being a young star athlete eventually paid for his college degree, changing his life forever. He was lucky; many of his friends didn't make it nearly this far.

"Whatever," he said "do me a favor, take some of my money and bring me a Max's pizza cheese steak when you come home."

"I will not," I said, "you can drive your lazy tail up to Broad and Erie just like I can." I said grabbing my purse exiting the bedroom.

"C'mon Meeka you're already headed up there. C'mon baby, a large…with extra sauce!!!" He yelled after me as I headed out of our Center City townhouse.

Jason, just like me was raised up on the north side of Philadelphia. He came from Nicetown and I grew up in Hunting Park. He went to Gratz for high school, and I went to Olney, but for the most part our upbringing was pretty much the same.

But somewhere after he graduated from Drexel and I from Temple, he got it in his head that he was somehow above the people he'd known all his life.

By the time we were married and our investment-consulting firm was solidly successful, Jason had completely turned his back on not just our old neighborhood but his old friends as well.

Not me, I never forgot where I came from. I knew that no matter where I could fly to from Philly International, no matter how many stamps I could get on my passport; my hood…was my home. It was so important to me that Jason tried to remember that we were fortunate, not better.

Not only were many of my friends and family there, so were my favorite memories, hangouts and my favorite foods. Sure we could afford to eat at Ruth Chris or McCormick and Schmidt's if we wanted, but sometimes I just didn't want to.

If I wanted ribs…I still went to Dwight's, crispy golden fried shrimp…it was either Sid Bookers or the El Dorado, if I wanted crabs…the Clock Bar was still right on time and when I wanted a good hoagie or cheesesteak…you couldn't beat Max's.

Jason and I frequented those spots for years together, until he became too high 'sidity for the old neighborhood. What I wouldn't do to have him sit side by side with me and enjoy and drink and some music in one of our old hangouts.

Tonight though, I was meeting Vanessa and Jamilah at the Eagle Bar for drinks. Vanessa worked for the parking authority and Jamilah drove a bus for Septa. It had been a few months since we'd caught up with each other and Vanessa wanted to stay local, so the Eagle was it.

I arrived there just a little past nine. Jamilah was already there sipping on a 'sex on the beach' her favorite drink. "What's shakin' momma?" Jamilah said sitting on a bar stool twirling her straw around with her long airbrushed acrylic nails. Jamilah, draped in gold jewelry, tight jeans and plunging black nylon shirt that unashamedly showed off Jamilah's double A bra cup breast, since God gave Jamilah all her curves below her waist. What she lacked in chest she definitely made up for it in butt.

Jamilah's skin was the creamy color of a freshly peeled banana with girly tattoos scribbled on her back, arms, wrist and chest. My girl J, had been wearing her hair cut short and dyed platinum blonde since high school, tonight it was brushed smooth on the sides with raised beveled curls on the top and back giving her the look of a faux Mohawk.

I joined her on the barstool and ordered a large Cosmopolitan; the Eagle had the tallest, most potent drinks you could imagine. Sipping on my cocktail, I listened while Jamilah gave me a rundown on the who, what, where and why of the neighborhood.

By the time she finished relaying who was pregnant, what Keesha found under her son's mattress, where Mookie from 12th Street got caught getting a blow job, and why she was leaving her boyfriend of ten years for the fourth time, Vanessa was walking through the door.

Vanessa was our sexy, thick chick of the group. Five foot, five, she was round everywhere; except for her little waist, which sat below two big jiggly breasts supported by round 'hug your momma' arms and flowed not three inches into a round curvy hips, butt and thighs. Vanessa had a pretty face, shoulder length dark hair, flawless chocolate toned skin and the brightest, whitest smile you'd ever seen. Big guys loved her for and despite her size; Vanessa had the longest list of over six foot tall boyfriends, despite the fact that she was going on her seventh year of marriage to her Puerto Rican husband Jose. "Hello Ladies, how ya'll doing?"

"Good." Both Jamilah and I replied together.

"Hope y'all don't mind, I told Muggy to meet me here later on." She said, straightening her denim mini skirt and matching halter-top.

Both of us shrugged. It was routine for Vanessa to meet up with her men on the side when we got together for ladies night, and as always she'd slip out a little early like twelve or twelve thirty, so that she could break her date off a little and still make it home before Jose was expecting her at two thirty.

Muggy was the captain of our high school football team back in the day. Vanessa and he had been kicking it since we were kids though they never became an official couple. Nowadays he worked for the sanitation department and lived in Germantown with his wife, mother-in-law and four kids.

Vanessa ordered her usual drink called a 'crazy muthafucka', which was a fruity concoction with many different types of liquors. Vanessa could only safely enjoy two maximum, before we'd have to carry her thick butt out of there.

We were having fun gossiping, drinking, enjoying the music and the lively atmosphere. We checked out every guy that walked through the door, if he was fine we'd give him his props, if he was corny we'd bust on his ass until the next guy walked through; same thing with the girls.

Every now and then a brother would pass by hit one of us with a line. If he wasn't buying drinks none of us even gave him a second glance. If he was buying drinks, he had to buy one for all of us. We'd flirt it up while waiting for our order and then once the drinks were served, we'd turn our backs and forget a brother was ever there, till he eventually got the point and moved on.

I was sipping on my second Cosmo when I noticed the fine specimen as he walked through the door. He was tall, dark and gorgeous. I recognized him immediately, but turned my head as if I didn't see him. 'Juice' was a guy I knew from back in the day; we had a history together. If there was ever someone I would call my old flame, Juice would be it.

He and I and I met in middle school, and were instantly an eighth grade item, as serious in love as you could possibly be at thirteen. My first love Juice was fine, a little hard around the edges, but sexy to the core.

He always looked great, even back in middle school. Even back then, he kept a fresh cut and his nails stayed clean and well trimmed. On top of that he had natural kind of charisma, people; especially girls, were drawn to him.

Tonight Juice was full grown hood. He had his grown man on in a big way, with a tailored striped shirt, a fresh pair of True Religion Jeans, Moschino sunglasses and brown Prada loafers. He wore a watch full of bling, a platinum necklace with a diamond pendant on it and a diamond stud in his right ear. His right hand was devoid of jewelry, but I couldn't help but notice the platinum wedding band he sported on his left hand.

It had been a while since I'd seen him like this, but my attraction for him was definitely still there. I silently cursed myself for the sexual tension that began building inside of me the moment he strolled through the door. He spotted me immediately, but cool ass Juice didn't play himself. He walked right past me up to the bar and ordered his drink. "Is that who I think it is?" Vanessa asked loudly.

"Mmm Hmm, that's him," I said sipping my drink, wondering how long it was going to take him to acknowledge me.

"Heyyyy Juice!" Jamilah said to him as the bartender handed him a Corona with the wedge of lime sticking up from the top of the bottle.

"What's up Mil?" Juice said coolly, still not looking in my direction. "That a new tattoo?" He asked looking at the blue butterfly on her shoulder.

"Mmm hmm, Ill Skilz did it."

"I like that, it's sexy."

"Hi Juice!" Vanessa said, wiggling in her chair, "long time, no see."

"Hey, Nessa." Juice said to her, "You look good girl, did you lose some weight?"

"Get outta here Juice you know I'm the same size I've always been." Vanessa said grinning from his compliment.

"Yeah well, you wear it well." Juice said, and without even facing him I knew by the sound of his voice that he was flashing that million-dollar smile of his that could make me melt.

I continued to keep my head turned; I wasn't going to say a word to Juice until he spoke to me first. "Girl, y'all need to stop fronting." Jamilah said whispering in my ear, "You know your glad to see him here, say hello to the man!"

"He sees me, just like I see him…he can speak too." I replied.

With that he came up behind me, "hello Tameeka." I heard Juice say in my ear.

'Damn he smells good', I thought catching a whiff of his cologne, it was John Varvatos one of my favorites. Without turning to face him I replied with a, "Hello Juice."

"Oh, who you talking to?" He teased me "The drink? The bar? What? 'Cause I'm right here." Juice said behind me.

I turned in my seat to face him, trying hard to suppress my smile, putting on my very best nonchalant face. "I said, hello Juice."

"That's better." He said seductively, standing too close for my composure. Just one look and that was it for me; I was a moth and he was bright light. Juice looked me up and down, from my hairstyle to my sling back sandals, and then made an expression as if to say he approved of the way I looked.

"Like what you see?" I said sarcastically.

"Mmm Hmm, love it." Juice said sipping from his beer, still taking in my form. I was certain he knew how much his gazing at my body was turning me on; he'd done it so many times before.

I could feel Jamilah and Vanessa's eyes on me; I knew they were enjoying this. "Hold my seat for me Juice, I gotta go to the ladies room," Jamilah said jumping off her bar stool.

"Me too girl." Vanessa said sliding off her seat as well. I stared after them for a moment seething because I knew they'd just set me up.

Juice sat down in the seat next to me but before he said anything else he raised a finger to hail the bartender and ordered a fresh round of drink for the ladies and me.

When he finally turned and faced me again, my knees were already jello, just from being this close to him. "It's good seeing you here, Tameeka."

"Yeah, it's good to see you here too," I said, still trying to compose myself. I took a long sip from my drink, hoping it would cool me off; no such luck. "I'm surprised to see you Juice, it's been such a long time." I said talking as low as the jumping music would allow me.

Juice slipped his arm around my waist a pulled me in a little closer. His hand rested just beneath my breast and held there. The touch from his hand instantly made my nipples rise beneath my shirt. I could tell he noticed right away. "You know," he said whispering in my ear, "I'm gonna have to have me, some of you before I say good night tonight."

It wasn't a question, not a suggestion; Juice was simply stating a fact. I twisted my face and tried to put on a disinterested expression, but I knew I was failing miserably. "What, no small talk Juice? No trying to find out if I'm even still feeling you like that?" I said trying to be offended by his cockiness.

"No need to, I know you're feeling me." he replied, his lips touching my ear as he spoke, "Hell, I'm Juice baby." His hand had risen up higher by now cupping my breast, his thumb teasing my nipple through the slinky fabric of my shirt.

"Whatever," I replied.

The bar was crowded with people, so no one really noticed as he slid his hand under my shirt and continued to toy with my breast beneath my bra. My breath caught when his thumb and forefinger gently pinched my nipple. He knew this would turn me on, my breast were always ultra sensitive. The more he toyed and pinched, the more I could feel my panties becoming wet as I wriggled slightly in my seat, my crotch pressing against the stitch in my jeans; reveling in the sensation of him touching me. Surprising even myself, I let out a soft moan.

"See, I told you…you're still feeling me." Juice said in my ear.

'Thank God' I thought to myself when the bartender placed our drinks in front of us and Vanessa and Jamilah returned from the ladies room.

"Y'all enjoying yourselves?" Jamilah asked as Juice returned her seat. Then eyeing the fresh round of drinks said, "Oh thank you Juice!"

"Thanks Juice!" Vanessa chimed in lifting her glass up from the bar. "Muggy baby!" she then said smiling, waving and looking towards the door.

Muggy and all of his six foot six frame walked over to us with a huge grin on his face. Muggy waited patiently while Vanessa finished her drink, then after a few minutes of hellos and sharing some dap with Juice, Vanessa and Muggy were headed out the door.

Jamilah had turned her attention to an older dude who was sitting on her other side. He was an old school daddy, dripping with gold and diamond jewelry, gold teeth, a loudly printed silk shirt, sunglasses and hat, complete with a pimp cane and all. Jamilah always had the weirdest taste in men.

That left me once again giving my full attention to Juice. "He don't have to know...she don't have to know", John Legend was singing dramatically through the sound system as Juice looked hard into my eyes. Sitting this close to him I recalled the times we'd run into each other like this in the past.

Though it had been a while, I still remembered the night at the Stinger, when we sat way in the back. Without being noticed by anyone in the club, Juice pulled me up on his lap and slid into me, stroking himself into me slowly, deliberately, making me come over and over again all night on his hardness right there in the club.

Then there was the time, we bumped into each other at the Tender Touch and he fingered me till I exploded all over his hands while seated at the bar. Then I dropped down beneath the bar and serviced him with a blowjob until he erupted all over my silk blouse.

My favorite episode was the night we ran into each other at Lou and Choo's and I followed Juice out to his ride where we sixty nined each other in the back of his Escalade.

I wondered what he had in store for us tonight, whatever it was I was game, though I tried not to let on how eager I was. Just as the thought hit me, Juice took me by the hand and said, "follow me." I could see in his eyes he was ready for me.

"I'll be back." I leaned in to tell Jamilah.

"No you won't hussy, I'll just call you tomorrow." Jamilah said knowingly, then sucked her teeth and said, "Y'all is just nasty." Grinning at us both before returning back to her Ronald Isley look alike.

Juice directed me towards the back of the bar, at first I thought he was going to take me to one of the rest rooms, and I wasn't at all for that, not after a night of drunken missed toilet aims.

But he didn't he slipped me out the back door and led me to his truck. I already knew not to ask where we were going. Part of the excitement is that Juice was always in control. "Jump in." he said holding the door for me and I did.

When Juice started up the engine, Gerald LeVert's voice came on over the sound system. Backing out of the parking space, his truck smoothly cruised up to the corner and he made a right hand turn onto Broad Street.

I was overcome with anticipation. I knew what I was in store for and I couldn't wait. Juice was going to touch me and my body was going to come alive with wanting him. We barely spoke a word as he drove north through four green lights before making a right hand turn onto Hunting Park Avenue. One block down and we were in the park.

Juice pulled over and unlocked our doors; coming around to my side he let me out. Without a word we began kissing passionately, Excited about being so close to him, I was barely aware of the danger of being in Hunting Park at night. Perhaps the police would sweep by and catch us, perhaps worse. I didn't care…all I cared about was the way Juice was roughly removing my bra as I slid out of my jeans tossing them to the ground.

As he tugged at my panties, tearing the thin satin ribbon that held the fabric together, memories of us being young teenagers making out in the same park on our way home from school strangely turned me on even more.

Our lips separated long enough for Juice to remove his shirt and open his jeans. While he pulled his penis out, he guided me down on my knees in the dirt and drew my face to him.

I eagerly drew him into my mouth sucking till he grew large enough in my mouth to gag me at the back of my throat. Hungry for him I swallowed him down deeper. Sliding my mouth up and down, I let the tip of my tongue trace the map of bulging veins, sucking loudly at the dip before filling my face again with him completely. Once I had him nice and hard, Juice pulled me up by my hair, "Get up," he commanded me.

As soon as I rose to my feet he roughly leaned me over the hood of his Escalade, my arms and face feeling the heat of his still warm engine radiating off the metal. I was wearing nothing now except my heeled sandals. Juice fell to his knees, used his two hands to part my ass cheeks open and began eating me both front and back, slurping loudly as his lips and tongue teased and pleased me.

I threw my hips backwards towards his mouth as he dove his tongue inside me deeper and deeper, his fingers probing me finding the spots that he knew would make me tremble.

I was close, so close when Juice removed his hands and face away, letting the warm summer air blow against my wet and exposed skin. Juice brought his open palm up and slapped my butt loudly, the sound echoing through the trees. When he rose to his feet, he wrapped one arm around my waist, and the other hand he used to guide himself into me as I stood there awaiting the feeling of him inside me.

When we connected, Juice raised that hand and placed it around my throat making me feel the pressure of his hand with each stroke between my legs.

"This is what you want right Tameeka." Juice said pounding into me hard, grunting deeply with each thrust.

"Yes Juice." I replied, barely able to talk from the pressure on my throat. Juice drew me by my waist even harder against his strokes making me scream out loud as he slipped in deeper. My knees felt ready to give way with each stroke, but I held on letting him take me over and over again till to the point where I began to feel dizzy.

Juice removed his hand from my throat and slid it down to one of my waiting nipples. Feeling completely, lightheaded, I greedily gulped in air, while he pinched my nipple again between his fingers. "Who gives it to you like this Tameeka?" Juice said in my ear while slapping me hard on my ass, making my cheeks sting and tingle with each strike.

"You Juice, only you!" I cried.

"Damn, right," he said satisfied with my answer. Juice turned me around, his back now leaning against the truck, leaving my nakedness exposed to the street traffic not many yards away. Oblivious to the car lights as they drove by, I bent my knees even deeper letting myself feel the violence of his every thrust.

Juice reached one hand around my waist and smacked me several times between my legs, gripping me with his palm between strokes. I tingled and stung all over, but every inch of me felt alive as I watched cars drive by not caring if they could see me through the park trees or not.

Juice bent me over and continued taking me doggy style, till I could barely feel my legs, but that didn't stop the tremors in my belly as I felt myself about to climax like crazy. When Juice felt my body tense up, he brought one hand around to the front rubbing me between his fingers until I shuddered in pleasure. "Juice!!!" I screamed as each thrust took me over the top.

Not moments after, Juice finally had all he could take, he pummeled into me even harder until his very last thrust. He held me tightly by the waist grinding his hips into me as he exploded in one pulsing wave after another. Even after he'd begun to soften, he remained inside, letting me feel the warm stickiness as it streamed past us both onto the patches of grass and dirt beneath our feet.

Spinning me around again Juice covered my face in kisses. We held each other tightly and as tender as we'd been rough moments before. "Oh Meeka" he said falling out of his thug character, "Meeka, I love you so much girl."

I looked my husband in the eyes; I knew he had to love me to do this for me. He knew I loved the thug he used to be, the rough boy he was back in the day. Only Jason would think up kinky scenarios that made me so hot, turned me on like crazy.

Working together side by side the way we did every day could make our marriage become routine, it was Jason falling into his Juice persona every now and then, that helped to keep things fresh…broke the monotony. Because of him our marriage never got stale.

Not that I didn't love my professional, BMW driving, Blackberry carrying, stock market watching, Wall Street Journal reading husband; there was just something exciting about the way he used to be. "I love you too Jason," I said.

"Juice baby, I'm still Juice for the rest of the night." He said helping me back into the rented Escalade.

"Does that mean?" I said smiling.

"Mmm Hmm," he said making the drive back to my car at the Eagle Bar. "Hurry up and get your ass home 'cause Juice is coming to see you tonight." Jason said slipping back on his sunglasses.

I giggled in anticipation, we'd never taken our role-play back home with us, this was something new and I could not wait. Excited I bounced towards my car, completely unaware of my dirty and disheveled clothes. Before Jason, pulled off in the truck he rolled his window down and yelled out to me. "And don't forget my pizza cheese steak Meeka…extra sauce!"

"Yes Juice!" I called back. Mmmph! I couldn't wait to get home!

The Stand Up...pt 1.

"That's it!" Iris said out loud to no one in particular as she sat at an outside table at The B. She sat there fuming stirring her ice around in her fourth ginger ale with a cherry to make it look like she was drinking alcohol.

This was the fifth time in two months that Cameron had stood her up and each time he had some ridiculous excuse. "Bullshit!" she said aloud again reading his text message that his child's mother called him over for an emergency, his little boy was sick so he was staying the night.

"If he's sick", she texted, "why don't you take him to the hospital?"

"Not that bad," he texted back a reply, "just here keeping and eye on him."

Iris hated how he used his son as an excuse, when she knew the truth was that Cameron still had feelings for his baby momma Jessica. 'They're probably still sleeping together' she thought to herself. Though Cameron would swear they were done with each other years ago.

His little boy was eleven years old already, yet Cameron still slept at least a third of his nights at Jessica's place, supposedly on his son's behalf.

"Where do you sleep, when you're over there?" Iris once asked him.

"On the couch," he replied, his eyes not meeting hers as he spoke.

"Mmm Hmm," was her response, letting it drop. But female intuition told her he was still playing house with Jessica. Iris was beginning to realize that she was little more than part time diversion, his little sex toy, more than anything else.

Even after two years, she knew that there was no real relationship going on between them, when he did decide to come around it was for sex and before she knew it, he was gone again.

Finishing her soda, she decided to use the bathroom before heading back down Main Street to her apartment right there in Manayunk. Iris stared at her reflection in the bathroom mirror. Why she couldn't find a man, who wanted to be committed to her, puzzled her.

It wasn't as if she wasn't attractive, standing five foot eight, golden complected with amber eyes and naturally curly brown hair, slim but curvy body and a prize winning set of thirty eight double d breast. Even Iris could admit she was really something to look at. Still she wondered as hot as she was why that never translated into finding a man she could be truly happy with. "Looks ain't everything, huh?" She asked her image in the mirror. Her reflection only stared back at her, offering no sympathy, no reply.

Inside the bar was jumping, a bunch of girls danced in the middle of the floor to the Pussycat Dolls, playing on the radio. *"Don't cha wish your girlfriend was hot like me…"* they sang loudly with their drinks in their hands.

A group of guys sat at the bar and watched as the drunken girls wiggled and gyrated to the music. Iris wished she were having fun like them, she was hoping that once she and Cam met up they would have a good time. But no, she was stood up once more, 'yeah, but for the last time', she promised herself.

Easing past the crowd Iris paid her tab and headed towards the door. Still annoyed with Cameron, Iris was distracted by her thoughts, and didn't notice the guy standing at the door; with his head turned; he didn't notice her as well. She was walking so quickly and his response was so slow, that their collision was unavoidable. Before either of them knew what was happening, their heads met together with a loud crack and both fell to the floor with a loud thump.

"Oh God I'm sorry!" The guy said first getting up then helping her to her feet. Looking around he realized hardly anyone had noticed their fall. Turning his attention back to Iris he saw that his drink had spilled all over her blouse. His first instinct was to brush off all the ice that had spilled onto her chest, realizing seconds too late, that it wasn't that great of an idea.

Iris was dazed, her head spinning a little. Feeling her forehead, she felt the sore patch as a swollen bump began to rise clear in the center. She said nothing trying to get herself together, but quickly came to when the strange guy's hands began brushing back and forth across her breast. "Hey, what the hell are you doing? Get your hands off of me!" She yelled over the music playing at in the bar.

"I'm sorry, I'm really sorry!" He repeated, his face looking embarrassed and concerned.

Iris looked at her assailant, her mood souring more with each passing second. He was just about six feet tall; in her heels he wasn't that much taller than she was. Looking into his piercing hazel eyes, she barely noticed his naturally tan skin, sandy colored closely cropped wavy hair, and neatly trimmed moustache; barely, but she noticed. In her anger she tried to remember the name of the actor he looked like, she couldn't put her finger on it, but she knew it was an actor from Philly.

He was wearing an oxford shirt and jeans, both as covered by his drink and ice and she was. On his forehead, he too was beginning to sport a sizable knot as well. That's when she realized he was just as hurt as she was and saw she owed him an apology as well. "Yeah, I'm sorry too." She offered.

"Can I buy you a drink?" He asked. Then realizing that perhaps drinking alcohol after a head butt like that maybe wasn't such a good idea added, "or maybe some fresh air, we could sit outside for a minute."

"No, no I was just leaving." Iris answered gingerly touching the sore spot on her head.

"Oh ok, " he said. If Iris wasn't mistaken he looked a little disappointed. "Can I at least hail down a cab for you?"

Iris had planned to walk home; her apartment was no more than ten blocks down Main Street right on the Schuylkill River. Feeling the wetness of her shirt and sure her head looked mess Iris decided he was right, it might be a good idea to catch a cab. She looked at the cute stranger again, he appeared to be sincerely sorry and his offer to hail a cab for her was really courteous.

Iris tried forcing a smile, it came to her lips eventually with some difficulty; she was still reeling from their accident and still furious with Cameron for standing her up.

"I'd appreciate that, thanks." She answered.

"Reese...Reese Foster." He said extending his hand. Iris noticed his eyes sort of sparkled when he smiled; his voice was smooth almost soft when he spoke.

"Iris Carter." She replied smiling sincerely this time.

"Well Iris, I'll see if I can get you home in one piece, I'll try my best to help since we both seem a little accident prone." He said giving her a warm smile.

Reese left her sitting there in a seat in the corner while he went outside to busy Main Street. He was back inside in less than ten minutes and was a moment later helping her into the back seat.

"Where to lady?" the cab driver asked.

After she gave him her address, Reese reached into his pocket and handed the driver a twenty-dollar bill.

"It's an eight dollar fare." The cab driver said, while tucking the twenty into his shirt.

"Keep the change." Reese replied.

"You didn't have to do that." Iris said when Reese reached in to give her a handshake goodbye.

"Least I can do, for that," he said pointing to the knot that was now full blown.

"Yeah well, you have one too." She replied touching his forehead gently.

"Meter running." The driver yelled back to them.

"Listen," Reese said. "Here's my card. Call and let me know you've gotten home safely.

Iris smiled, "I'll do that Reese."

The cab got her home in less than ten minutes even with the busy traffic on Main Street. Once inside her apartment, Iris poured herself a glass of wine, filled a zip lock bag with ice for her head and headed straight to her bedroom to undress, shower and lie across the bed for another night of television. Normally she would do at least a half hour of yoga before going to bed, tonight though she decided to skip it.

After sliding into a comfortable t-shirt and soft cotton panties, Iris remembered Reese' card in her purse. She quickly dialed his number. When his voicemail came on with the first ring she left him a brief message thanking him again and telling him she'd made it home safely.

Lying back in her bed she applied the bag of ice to her forehead, it didn't hurt as much as it had earlier and the swelling seemed to be going down with the ice. She wondered how Reese was making out with his, and then she just wondered about Reese. At the bar she didn't have much time to think about him, but had her head not been hurting she probably would have been seriously checking him out.

He was cute to say the least; Iris wondered what he was doing standing there by the door all alone that way anyway. 'Perhaps he was waiting for someone too', she figured.

All alone in her apartment, her mind traveled back to Cameron and their apparent non-relationship. She wondered why she put so much stock in Cameron when he'd done nothing but disappoint her since they'd met.

But she knew why. As unavailable as Cameron was, when they did get together it was amazing, and sex with Cameron was simply earth shattering. He taught her things she'd never before tried and she let Cameron go places no man had ever gone.

Just thinking about him now and the first time they experimented with tantric sex got her excited. Cameron came to her place with books and cd's on erotic chanting. At first all that stuff weirded her out, but when she tried it and he began taking her to new heights she was an instant believer. 'Sex', Cam told her "according to the Kama Sutra supposed to be as spiritual as it was physical."

The incense, music, oils, massages and dozens of positions kept sex fun and purposeful. Cameron knew how to incite all her senses long before he brought her to one exquisite orgasm after another.

There was so much she knew now, he'd patiently taught her the art, and after two years time she had mastered everything Cameron knew and more, she could actually teach someone else by now if she chose to.

Now if only he put that kind of effort into being available and she suspected faithful as well, he'd been one hell of a boyfriend. Iris laid there in bed thinking about all of the erotic positions he would put her in.

"Union of the Cow" Cam would say, and she automatically would draw up on her knees and let him enter her from behind. "Union of the Tiger" and he was above her with her legs wrapped high around his elbows.

Iris lay there in bed thinking about all of them, getting herself excited with each thought. 'Position of the Courtesan' was her favorite position of all. It put her in a power position on top with her back facing him while he slid himself deep inside her.

Her thoughts were turning her on, moving her hips a little while under the covers she could feel her panties becoming damp and decided to take them off, then decided to let the t-shirt follow as well. She quickly grabbed her remote and shut the television off too.

Lying there in the darkness of her room, beneath her covers, Iris let her hands take a journey all over her body, caressing her full breast, toying with her nipples even drawing the left one in her mouth and sucking it.

Her hands moved lower, stroking the soft skin of her belly, hips and thighs. Raising her legs and opening them wide, she reached behind her with one hand caressing the smooth skin of her butt while teasing the wetness between her legs with the other.

'Mmmm", she moaned to herself as one finger, than two slipped past her shaved mound and found themselves inside. Iris rocked her hips back and forth, enjoying the feeling as her fingers slid in and out and her thumb toyed gently against her swollen nub.

Iris let her mind take her back to the night when he first taught her how to prepare for Tantric sex by doing yoga daily, and still she faithfully bent and twisted her body in the same series of stretches every morning and night to ensure she stayed as limber and flexible for him as she could.

That flexibility was paying off now as she drew one leg so high towards her chest, that she could slip one moistened index finger in her tight hole from behind while still sliding her two fingers from the other hand in front.

Iris was turning herself on from her own double penetration, moving her hips down against both of her hands. Looking down at her own breast as they jiggled and bounced from her own movements making her even hotter. She loved watching as the cocoa colored circles of her areola bounced back and forth towards each other.

Iris loved her body and wished she had a mirror over her bed like Cameron did so that she could see how sexy she looked while she pleasured herself.

Feeling herself close to cresting, she moved her hands even more insistently, anticipating the feeling of her oncoming orgasm. Her fingers and thumb moved feverishly as her breath quickened and then caught.

Holding her breath she felt herself tense just for a moment and then a flood of release flowed making her fingers slick with her coming.

Iris let herself rest for a moment though fully aware that she wasn't yet satisfied. When she was able to compose herself, she reached for the little satin pillow on the side of her bed. Slipping her hand inside the little velvet lined compartment she pulled out her vibrator.

It looked more like a child's toy than anything else. Her toy was baby blue covered in soft rubber latex and shaped somewhat like the swirls on a soft serve ice cream cone. But when she turned it on, like she was doing now it was her boyfriend whenever Cameron was unreachable.

Tonite 'boyfriend' was going to take good care of her. Iris started out on a low speed letting her excitement build, rubbing the tip against her still sensitive clit, once again she moved her hips, moaning enjoying the feel of the latex as it slid across her slippery skin. Sliding half it inside, she rode against it, closing her eyes imagining it was Cameron taking his time entering her.

Pushing the tip further inside, she let the base press against her clit as she slid in and out slowly. Turning up the speed on the little knob at the base she squeezed her eyes tightly letting her imagination run wild.

Iris tried picturing herself with Cam like she'd normally do, but before she knew it, mental picture of him changed to a face of another guy; it was Reese from the bar.

She pictured him licking her, sucking her; bending her in various positions. In her imagination Iris was making love to Reese and he expertly made love to every inch of her body.

The little movie playing in her head was setting her on fire, turning her on with images of scenes she knew she would probably never play out in real life. But in her own little fantasy world the sex with Reese was amazing.

She was close to her second orgasm when her phone rang. She reluctantly turned off the vibrator, and picked up her Blackberry. Not recognizing the number she thought perhaps Cameron was calling her from a different telephone number, no one else really called her this late at night, "Cam?" she said her voice sounding breathy from still being so turned on.

"Uh, no it's me Reese."

It took several seconds for her to speak, startled that he called right in the middle of her fantasy of him "Oh ok, Reese from the bar," she said, 'hi.'"

"Did I catch you at a bad time?" He asked.

Iris realized how her voice must have sounded, deep and seductive; her fuck voice. Clearing her throat she tried lifting her voice an octave or two to sound a little more cheerful. "No, not at all, I was just lying here watching television," she lied. The TV was off by now, and she hadn't once looked at it. "I tried calling you."

"Yeah I know I got your message, my cell phone battery had died, I had to charge it up when I got home," he answered, then "listen, I have your wallet here."

"My wallet?" Iris asked wondering what he was talking about.

"Yeah, I guess you dropped it when we bumped into each other, the bartender thought you were my girlfriend and handed it to me when I got back to the bar." Reese said.

Iris jumped out of bed and checked her purse, and sure enough her little wallet that held her ID, a few credit cards, her health insurance card and about thirty dollars in bills was missing. She wondered how in the world she made it home without noticing. Then it hit her, Reese paid for the cab, and she never had to open her purse except to take out his card once she got home. "Oh my god Reese, your right."

"Do you want me to drop it in the mail for you?" Reese asked.

Iris noted again how smooth his voice sounded, it was soft and sensual, and her nipples responded by tightening at the sound of him as he spoke. She blushed thinking of her fantasy not minutes before. "Umm no, I'll need it before it could arrive in the mail. Maybe we could meet somewhere."

"I heard you tell the driver your address, I'd be happy to drop it off at your building."

She thought about it for a moment, Reese didn't appear to be threatening in any way; Iris figured that would be ok. "Is that a far drive for you?"

"No," he replied "actually, I live at the opposite end of Main Street from you."

"Those new condos?" It was an upscale complex set in renovated historic factory buildings. The Watermill was an architectural dream, very sleek interiors, very Sharper Image. Iris remembered hearing they'd opened. She even considered buying one till she saw how much they were selling for. 'Maybe in a few years,' she'd thought.

"Yeah, I'm not that far at all." Reese answered.

"Tell you what, I'll meet you downstairs in lets say ten minutes, ok?" Iris said, surprising herself at how excited she was to see him again.

"Sounds good, see you then." He said.

"And Reese…thanks." Iris said hanging up the line. Twice tonight he'd looked out for her. First the cab, then making sure she got her wallet. Iris had no idea it was even missing; she shuddered to think what would have happened had it gotten in the wrong hands.

Sliding 'boyfriend' back into her 'hide a vibe' pillow, her little love session between herself and the imaginary Reese, would have to wait till later. Freshening up, she quickly dressed throwing on hip hugging sweat pants, a sleeveless tank and slide on slippers. Checking her reflection, she decided to brush her still damp hair and touch up her lip-gloss and mascara. "You never know," she said out loud to herself feeling a little excited.

She thought about Cameron, she was getting pretty fed up with his lying to her, doubting very much that he was lying on a couch anywhere right now. Thinking about Reese, she caught herself wondering what he was like, what were his interest, what did he like to do. Perhaps they're little accident was not and accident but their fate to meet.

Just minutes before she was to see Reese downstairs, she decided to dim the lights in her apartment, scatter a few silk scarves about her richly colored living room, light a few candles and incense, and put on a 'Songs of Devi" cd. "You never know." She said again, thinking if the vibe was right, she may decide to invite him in.

Looking around satisfied, Iris headed out the door and taking the stairs down a flight to meet Reese. He was already there waiting for her. "Hey," Reese said handing her the wallet, looking her over again in the bright light.

"Hey yourself," she replied, slipping the wallet in her sweat pants pocket. Then looking at his red and still very swollen forehead said, "Ooh, it's gotten bigger huh?"

Reese touched his fingers delicately to his forehead. "Yeah, and it hurts like hell." He said sounding like a wounded little boy.

"Did you put ice on it?" Iris asked.

"No, was I supposed to?" Reese asked sincerely.

"Yeah, that would have taken care of that swelling, see mine is going down already."

"Wow, it is." Reese said pulling his gaze away from Iris' eyes to look at the lump on her forehead. It had gone down considerably and wasn't nearly as red at it was at the bar.

Iris smiled at him, charmed that he seemed so helpless and she had to admit even cuter than he was before. The vibe with him was definitely good. Reaching out her hand she took him by his hand. "C'mon, I'll take you up to my place…put a little ice on it for you."

"I hate to be a bother."

"Trust me," was her reply, "you won't be", she said guiding him up the stairs to her place."

The *Stand Up...pt 2.*

"That's it!" Reese said out loud to no one in particular as he stood in the crowded bar, barely sipping on his drink. He was really getting tired of trying to work it out with Stacey, when she obviously wasn't worried about working things out with him.

It bothered him that their relationship had gotten so bad, they argued almost every time they were together, mostly over how much money she was spending or how many nights she spent partying with her girlfriends. Eventually Reese had enough and moved out.

But Reese missed his little girls, maybe Stacey a little bit too. He couldn't honestly say he was in love with her, but he'd gotten used to being in a relationship with her, so no matter how much she got under his skin he thought it would be worth a try.

Sure he could see his daughters whenever he wanted to, but he missed waking up in the same house where they got dressed for school in the morning. He missed being there to help them with their homework at night. Reese was lonely and he missed having a family.

Against his better judgment, he'd planned to ask Stacey to move into his new place with him along with his daughters. It was a lot nicer than the old house they'd shared and Stacey still lived in with the girls up in Germantown. He'd just have to put his foot down with Stacey when it came to money, since that was their biggest problem.

Down here in Manayunk, his new place boasted plenty of room for all of them and it was still close to the girls' school. And there were all the places Stacey could shop at all along the Main Street strip; and Stacey loved spending his money…a little too much.

There were plenty of activity here for the girls as well, a park, and ice cream shop, art galleries, even a dance studio where he imagined his girls taking ballet. He and Stacey would just have to figure out a way to make it work; he thought about them getting counseling.

But, Stacey hadn't shown up again or even called to say she couldn't make it. It wasn't till hours later did she return his call to tell him she was out celebrating in Atlantic City at one of her girlfriend's bachelorette party.

"I thought we were getting together tonight Stac?" Reese said annoyed in the phone.

"Oh shit, Reese, I forgot." Stacey said not sounding too concerned.

'Bet she didn't forget to take my American Express card', he thought. "Stacey, I confirmed to night with you three times, how in the world could you forget?"

"Oh my God Reese, please don't be such a baby! We can hang out any time." She yelled into the phone over the sound of techno music and screaming women in the background.

'Probably at another one of those male stripper clubs.' He thought to himself. "I'm not being a baby, you and I really need to talk Stacey" he said, "my time is just as valuable as yours, you could have just called if you weren't gonna make it."

"Woo Hoo!" Stacey screamed into his ear, "Yeah baby, take it off!"

"Stac, did you hear what I said, the least you could have done was call!" Reese said sounding frustrated.

"Ok ok, 'Hello Reese, I'm not gonna make it tonight. Are you happy now?" Stacey asked sarcastically. Reese could almost picture her tossing her three hundred dollar weave around as she spoke.

"No not really, not that you care at all." Reese said furious with her for blowing him off once again.

"Yeah well, it'll have to be next weekend, 'cause I won't be home till Sunday night Deidre booked a suite, were gonna party all weekend." She said, sounding more than a little drunk.

Next weekend, was his weekend with the girls he had plans to drive them up to Rochester, New York to visit with his parents; his mother's birthday was on Saturday. Stacey knew that which meant she had no intentions to see him then either. Then he thought about his daughters, "Where are the girls Stacy?"

"They're fine, they're with my mother. Listen Reese gotta go, I need to get me some more singles, Woo Hoo!" She yelled in his ear once more before hanging up on him.

'Yeah, with my money' Reese thought, once again beating himself up for ever getting involved with her. Stacey was once his trophy girl, when he was still young he thought that real success meant having one of everything that would make the average guy eat his heart out; including the most beautiful woman he could find.

And Stacey was fine, gorgeous on the outside, but in time he learned she was vacant of anything of real value on the inside. He dated her because most of his buddies would have killed to have a girlfriend so fine.

He was so young then; fresh out of law school and at the time had something to prove. His tastes in women had evolved since then, and though he still loved beautiful women he understood a real woman had substance, she had depth; she at least had a job. She had everything that Stacey was completely devoid of.

She dated him, because his money ran freely. Stacey shopped and spent every dime she got her hands on, on designer anything. She loved her Marc Jacob bags more it seemed than she ever loved him.

Before he realized how bad her habit was, Stacey was close to delivering their second child. By then she'd almost ruined him financially; now he somewhat kept her on a tight budget, but not so tight that his girls would suffer.

Reese stood at the front door of the bar, pissed with her, pondering why he even let himself procreate with someone as ignorant as she. If it weren't for his daughters he wouldn't give Stacey a second thought. "That's the last time she's going to stand me up," he promised himself.

It was then, that he noticed the fine girl with a 'hellified' body walking towards him. He was so busy looking at the way her top fit her ample chest and her hips as they swung back and forth in her jeans that he didn't step back in time to let her past. Before his feet could register to move, they collided into each other, practically knocking her and himself out in the process.

He cringed thinking about how he'd made a fool of himself brushing his hands across her boobs right there in the bar. He was lucky she didn't slap him in the face. But as it turned out, she was nice about the whole thing; she even apologized to him.

When they introduced themselves, she said her name was Iris, incredibly beautiful Iris. Reese felt like a total idiot, here he was stressing out about his daughters' mother who obviously did not want him, when beautiful girls like Iris were walking around. Maybe it was time to put Stacey where she wanted to be on the back burner; perhaps it was time for him to think about moving on.

His forehead was hurting like hell; he could only imagine what hers felt like. Feeling bad once again he offered to hail a cab for her, the least he could do was make sure she got home ok.

Reese wanted to ask her for her phone number before the cab pulled off but decided to give her his card instead. 'Perhaps she'd call perhaps not' he thought heading back into the bar for one last drink before he went home for the night. His new place was only blocks away, so he'd be there in minutes.

It was strange luck that someone had turned her wallet in to the bartender, neither one of them noticed it fall. Even stranger that the bartender mistook them to be a couple, 'maybe it was an omen', he thought.

On his way home he thought even more about how pretty Iris was and how unusual that name was for a girl like her, but somehow her name fit; she was as pretty and exotic as the flower was. 'Yeah', he thought, 'I could see myself with her'.

Back at his place he stared at Iris' driver's license thinking how even on her id picture she looked good. Just like him she looked as if she had something heavy on her mind back there at the bar, Reese wondered what it was.

Reese assumed she'd never called to say she was ok, so he let it go. He'd planned to send her wallet back to her by mail after all it wasn't as if he'd made a great impression on her. But, after checking his messages he realized she had called him not long after the battery died on his phone.

Listening to her voice, Reese knew he had to see her again. Just as he had hoped she'd invited him to her building when he called her back. Before heading there he quickly rinsed his mouth with mouthwash and sprayed cologne on his shirt. "You never know", he said to his reflection before exiting his condo.

Reaching Iris' building he waited for her in the first floor lobby, when she came down and he really had a chance to see her in the light, she took his breath away.

Even in sweats she looked good; her skin was radiant almost flawless, her long brown curly hair hanging freely around her face made her look sweet, fresh and natural. Iris' golden amber eyes shone as she talked, lighting up as she smiled, as for her breast straining the thin t-shirt; Reese had to force himself not to stare.

He thought he'd hit the jackpot when she invited him up to her place. Entering the apartment was on a whole other level. Reese thought he had been transported to maybe India or the Middle East somewhere.

Iris' walls were of all colors, deep red. The pictures hanging on her walls and rugs were covered with colorful prints. Her windows sofa and chairs were draped with silk fabric, colorful scarves and brightly colored pillows casually placed about the room.

Never in a million years would he have guessed this was her place. Reese almost expected belly dancers to come from another room and entertain him.

Iris had candles of every sort burning throughout the room. The room itself smelled like rich wood and fragrant oils, looking in the corner he saw the scent came from burning incense. On her sound system played what sounded like women chanting and moaning.

This was definitely different from anything he'd ever seen before; Reese absently wondered what Iris was into. Iris offered him a seat while she went into the kitchen to get the ice for his head. When she returned she looked at his expression and offered an explanation. "I'm kinda fascinating with a lot of eastern cultures, hence the colors." She said with a shrug.

"I see," Reese said.

"So what do think?" She asked standing above him.

Reese wondered if she meant herself or the décor. She was a must have, and the décor was pretty cool too. He figured he'd be safer commenting on the décor. "It's exotic, I like it," he said honestly.

"Well thank you." Iris said joining him on the sofa. "Now hold still, this is going to be really cold." She said before placing the bag of ice on his forehead.

Even with the warning Reese jumped a little from the cold, but he held still while she applied the ice bag to his head. The sound of the women chanting and moaning once again filled his head. He just had to ask, "what kind of music is this?"

"It's more like a prayer than music," she answered. "It's a song to Devi."

"Whose is Devi?"

"Hindu's believe she's the Goddess. If everything in nature is a balance of man and woman, Devi is the female part of Divinity."

"Do you believe it?" Reese asked, curious to hear her answer.

Iris shrugged again, "I love the concept, it makes sense to me. But do I worship her, no not really. I'm open minded, but not really religious that way."

"Oh." Was all Reese could say, to be honest with himself he was more intrigued by the way her plump nipples showed through her t-shirt than learning about a goddess; as far as he was concerned the 'goddess' what right there before him. Reese was once again taken back by how gorgeous she was. Reese decided to change the subject before Iris noticed the beginning of an erection in his jeans. "You looked like something was on you mind tonight at the bar, is everything ok?" He asked.

Iris sighed a deep worried sigh, "My boyfriend, or should I say soon to be ex boyfriend stood me up again tonight." She said still leaning towards him holding the ice pack to his head. "What about you, you looked a little intense yourself."

Reese laughed a hollow chuckle, amazed at the coincidence. "Would you believe my ex girlfriend stood me up too?"

Iris sat at his side, thinking for a moment. "Don't you hate that?" Iris asked.

"What?"

"Loving somebody who doesn't love you back." Iris said, all at once understanding that was the basis of her relationship with Cameron, he liked her, even craved her; but Cam did not love her.

"Now that you put it that way; yeah, I'm tired of it." Reese answered. "I was planning to ask her to get back together at least for our kids." Reese sighed. "I'm kind of glad she never showed, I almost made the biggest mistake of my life twice."

"You two have kids together?" Iris asked, thinking 'here we go again.'

"Yup, two girls seven and nine." Reese answered.

Baby momma drama was a sore topic for Iris so she treaded lightly with her next question, "Let me ask you something."

"Shoot." Reese replied.

"Let's say the two of you never get back together. Would you; I mean; is it normal for a man spend several nights a week at his ex's house, to be close to his kids?"

"No way in Hell!" Reese said shaking his head empathetically, "If we're done; which I think we are; then we're done. I've already made sure they both have really nice rooms at my place. When it's time for them to be with me, my daughters are always welcome in my home."

"Hmm. Okay." Iris said considering his answer, which is what she would have figured as well. It just felt good to hear a man say that spending night after night at a woman's home that you were supposed to be over and done with, was an 'out of the question' idea. She made up her mind, good lover or not, Cameron and his lying tail was as good as yesterday. "That's enough about exes, lets toast to new friendships", Iris said.

"What are we toasting with?" Reese asked.

Iris thought for a minute, then after placing Reese's hand up to hold the ice pack, went to the kitchen to check. Returning with two glasses of cola, she'd drank the last of her wine earlier that night. "Sorry I don't have anything stronger," she apologized.

"No, this is cool," Reese said. "To new friends," as he raised his glass.

"To new friends!" Iris said and in her mind thought 'and goodbye to old ones!' Placing the drinks down on coasters, Iris checked Reese' forehead once again, the redness had gone away and the lump was starting to shrink as well. While leaning over him and tending to his bruise, she didn't realize that she had one of her breast lying all over his left shoulder as she leaned on him.

Her full breast were tempting, so tempting. Reese wanted so badly to reach out and feel them. Iris caught him watching and smiled. Feeling the weight of her soft breast against his shoulder sent a rush of heat to his face and shot a quick message down to the man in his pants, that a beautiful woman with a sexy body was practically all over him.

Reese didn't want to look like a horny young boy to Iris, so he chose to try and play it cool. Reese turned his gaze away reluctantly searching her colorful apartment for some kind of diversion.

What his eyes came upon was some type of wall hanging, at first he couldn't make out the images in the little window panes of what looked like some type of intricate poster, but and as he looked closer he realized the abstract people were couples in different sexual positions.

Iris saw him watching and offered, "it's a chart of the positions of the Kama Sutra, the ancient Indian art of love making,"

"Yeah I've seen them before." Reese said his concentration split between the pictures and Iris who was now getting up to refresh the ice pack. His mind instantly filled with images of Iris posing in each of the dozens of positions illustrated there.

"Which ones do you like?" Iris asked looking very interested.

Reese rose up from his chair and went to her poster, to his surprise it was made of finely woven fabric and not photo paper as he first assumed. Each image was carefully sewn in, the detail amazing. Gazing all around taking each of the sixty-four images in, Reese finally decided on three that appealed to him the most. "Yab Yum? Am I saying that right?"

"Mmm Hmm, the woman seated on her man, her legs wrapped around his waist, his legs folded beneath her, both of her arms leaning back supporting her while he guides her in." Iris said, standing behind him as he examined the chart.

"Svanka," Reese said. "I really like that one."

"Doggy style, huh?" Iris said standing even closer now.

"And, I think I like, Bamboo." Reese said turning to face her.

Iris caught his gaze and instantly recognized the want in his eyes. She thought about the irony, both of them stood up by their supposedly significant others and like fate they crossed paths; bumped heads, literally. Now here they were, at one o'clock in the morning, standing in front of her Kama Sutra chart, her intuition told her he was meant to be here. Gazing back into his eyes she said, "Me on my back, with one leg wrapped around your shoulder, guiding you in deeper." Iris said gazing into his eyes. "Yeah, I like Bamboo too."

Reese gazed into her eyes in wonderment; she was so young, so sexy and so…freaky. "How do know all of this?"

Iris hesitated, determined not to even mention Cameron's name. "I used to have a very good teacher." She said with the color rushing to her face, then, "but I guess I know enough now to teach someone else, someone special."

They were standing so close; Reese could smell the scent of her perfume. So close it would have been a shame not to take it further; so he did. "Would you like to teach me?" he asked.

"What? Bamboo?" She asked.

"All of it, teach me whatever it is you know." Reese said sincerely.

Iris looked into the pebbled flecks in his eyes and knew more than anything she wanted to be his teacher; not just a one-night stand, but truly a patient and thorough teacher of the beautiful arts of lovemaking; just like Cameron had been hers. "There is a lot more to this just these positions here on the wall."

"Yeah, but they're a start." Reese said his eyes pleading, his hands dying to touch her.

"It could take weeks, even months to teach you everything…" Iris replied, feeling herself getting warm.

Reese leaned in to kiss her, one hand wrapping around her waist, the other cupping her left breast through her shirt enjoying the softness and fullness of it. "I'm not going anywhere," he told her knowing he planned to be around this woman a hell of a lot longer than a few weeks, "we have all the time in the world."

Iris let herself enjoy his kiss once more, savoring the sweetness of his lips, the smoothness of his skin. She instantly wondered what the rest of him would feel like on her lips. Slowly slipping out of her clothes she kept her eyes fixed on Reese as she removed each item.

Reese never breaking eye contact followed suit, removing everything from his shirt to his shoes until they both stood there naked.

Iris let her eyes absorb his body, his entire physique getting her approval, from his lean sculpted arms and chest and nicely shaped ass to even his rather pretty looking feet. She definitely liked him physically. Absently she wondered what he was like as a person. 'First things first' her body told her as she found herself craving the feel of his body.

Reaching in for another kiss, Reese let himself savor the taste of her mouth, the feel of her tongue as she took control of him. Separating long enough to take in her body, he was thrilled with what she had to offer, mentally noting that her full breast and perfectly flat belly with the dangling piercing in her navel were probably his favorites.

"The object of Tantric love," she began while trailing her fingers up and down his smooth chest, is to join two bodies into one complete state of joy. You become me, I become you, we become one." She said now taking him into her hand. Iris let her hands stroke him, enjoying the feel of his skin in her palms she looked deeply in his eyes.

Reese let his hand slip between her legs toying with her, anticipating the moment he'd find himself buried between. "One, huh?" He said breathing deeply.

"Mmm Hmm, one." Iris replied leaning closer towards his hand.

"How do we become…one." Reese asked his eyes now almost closed, peering at her through his long eyelashes.

"Completely surrender ourselves to the pleasure of the other. There should be nothing the two of us wouldn't do to bring the other to total ecstasy." She replied, and then to demonstrate, she fell slowly to her knees, taking him into her mouth and sucking him gently until he was completely hard.

Reese stood there astonished and aroused, wanting to latch his fingers into her curls, understanding what she meant, he was ready to do anything it took to make that magnificent body of hers satisfied. Iris stayed there between his legs, sucking and drawing him in. When she was satisfied with his thickness she tore open a condom package and without using her hands slowly drew the condom down his length with the suction of just her mouth and secured it in place with her lips.

Then she took him by his hand and guided him down to the floor with her. "Let's start with your favorites"; she said reaching for a condom. "Yab Yum" she said climbing into his lap, guiding him into her slowly.

"Mmm, Yab Yum." Reese said bringing one of her nipples to his mouth with one hand and drawing her body down onto him completely with the other. Together they began a gentle see saw motion, Reese lifting her body slightly with each stroke.

Iris breath slowed down to match the pace of Reese' while she let him take control of their rhythm, momentarily forgetting who was the teacher and who was the student.

When Reese leaned his body back and moved his hip around in small circles, Iris gasped as pleasure coursed through her. Feeling his intensity growing in his controlled stokes, she moved her hips more deliberately towards him, wrapping both of her arms around him. Reaching in for another kiss, her tongue caressed his bottom lip, then the top as she tasted his mouth feeling how soft and sensual his lips felt against hers.

Reese drew her up and then let her bounce back down on him with each stroke as her legs tightly wrapped around him and held him in securely, enjoying the feel of her ass as it jiggled and smacked against his lap, and loving the view of her pretty breast as they bounced against his chest.

With each plunge Iris maneuvered herself to draw as much of him in as she could then as he lifted her up she pulled her muscle so tight inside that she could make her body suck and pull on him even harder then her mouth did before. How something so soft, warm and juicy could have so much control was beyond him, Reese was awestruck that her muscles were so well trained down there that she could latch onto him and grip him like a vise.

When her legs squeezed even tighter Reese knew she was preparing to come and he leaned back even further letting her take all of him inside.

Iris began a low moan as she thrust against him with each rush of pleasure as it flowed through her body to his, her body jerking against him with each flood of release. Reese in turn let himself release along with her, not completely, just enough for her to feel his own pulsations between them.

After a while, her rapid movements slowed down to a soft grind and then ceased altogether. Still holding each other tightly Iris whispered in Reese's ear, "So, what do you think of Yab Yum?"

"I like it," he said eager for more, still rock hard as she continued to sit on him.

"You're a fast learner," she said looking into his eyes. Knowing now that waiting on Cameron was no longer necessary.

"You're a great teacher," he said smiling, completely forgetting about Stacey.

"Ready for your next lesson?" Iris said smiling.

"I'm ready." Reese said

Iris rose from his body, sliding off of his hardness. Gathering a pile of satin pillows she reclined on her back raising one leg high and wide up in the air.

Reese's eyes first fell between her legs, noticing how much her flower resembled the one in which she was named and was compelled to taste her. As his tongue explored her trailing circles and sucking her gently making his face wet with her juice. Iris wiggled as twisted thrilled that he knew how to taste her the way she liked. When she trembled this time, it was soft gentle and sensual.

By now she had raised her leg higher, almost parallel to her ear. Iris smiled seductively, her right forefinger motioning for him to enter her, inviting him in. Reese gazed into her eyes excitedly as he slid on a second condom, already ready for their next session; astonished by her seductive pose; he'd never seen a sexier invitation. This woman was sensual and erotic, but there was something else there too. This was just casual sex and he knew that, but something inside him told him that things between the two of them had the potential to go a lot deeper. He was certain Iris was looking for exactly what he was looking for, a lover with purpose.

Iris gazed back as he climbed on top of her. Still looking in the sparkle of his eyes, Iris realized some meeting were by chance, some were destiny; something inside her told her Reese was going to be a whole lot more to her than just her student in the art of lovemaking. Even now she realized that something deep inside her seemed to click into place with him here, something right.

But for now she was enjoying the hell out of being his Kama Sutra teacher. Guiding him in for their second round, she said, "Baby, now I'm gonna teach you all about Bamboo."

The Substitute

Hazel was so, grateful she was able to leave the hotel chain negotiations a day early, Hawaii or not she was getting tired of conducting one boring meeting after another. Her client; a major hotel line was negotiating to buy out a smaller unsuccessful Hawaiian hotel resort whose seventies era tiki bar, luau, Don Ho style entertainment was now way past it's prime. Modern Hawaii was young and trendy, their only visitors now were the elderly who had been coming there for over forty or more years, but they drew no new clientele.

Hazel's client saw the vision of tearing down the old resorts and building newer more exciting super clubs with golf courses on the twenty-three acre beachfront lot. Linking two other super clubs on each side together on the small island's strip of beach, making for a more scenic and lucrative tourist attraction.

They kept trying to hold out in hopes of sweetening the pot. It was Hazel's job as a contract negotiator to help them see that they were already getting a better deal than their company was worth and that holding out was only serving to make her clients bored. Pretty soon if the deal did not close her client was going to move on. Once she helped the smaller chain realize they were fighting a losing battle, she was able to wrap up the details and head back home early.

The moment she could book one she caught a flight back to the mainland, stopping briefly at her Los Angeles office and then returning to LAX to catch a direct flight from LA straight to Philly International.

Her plane touched down at nine thirty pm, by ten pm she was in her BMW and headed home. A career in corporate takeovers could sometimes be tough, true she was a success and made excellent money helping the big fish eat the little fish, but having clients all over the country who wanted their hands and their company's money held carefully kept her away from home most of the time.

Her schedule had been so hectic lately that she barely saw her husband Ramsey at all. Ramsey, an established oil painter; worked from home. Years ago they hired an architect to design an elaborate art studio for him right there on their property, the thousand foot studio was converted from the hundred year old estate's carriage house. So only for the occasional off site project would Ramsey ever need to leave the comfy confines of their beautiful Chestnut Hill estate.

She loved her work, though she knew that Ramsey missed her badly when she was gone. Lately Ramsey had been urging her to open her own office if not at home than close by; maybe even consider a change in career. But Hazel had a goal, she didn't want to switch gears until her net worth was at the five million dollar mark, the goal used to be a million but she conquered that in the first ten years of her career. She promised Ramsey when she hit her goal, she'd slow down a little and so far she was just about half way there.

But she missed her husband too, Hazel couldn't remember the last time they actually sat down to a dinner table together; and forget about catching up on day-to-day events, by the time they could even pause to have a conversation several weeks had already passed. Hazel tried to remember the last time they'd made love, it was currently mid July and best she could remember they had one interlude several months back on Valentine's day, before then at Christmas and perhaps her birthday the October before. Only three times in over nine months; 'wow' she thought, 'time flied'.

She smiled thinking of how good her marriage was, and how good it was to be married to a man who understood her passion and her vision for her career. Patient Ramsey never once complained or gave her a hard time about her hectic schedule; after all he knew how important her goals were and agreed that in the long run it was best for the both of them. He never even complained about her not wanting children though she knew for a while at least that he wanted them badly. A career like hers took focus and children would only serve to draw her focus away.

Tonight she planned to fix all of that Ramsey was more than due for some love and attention. First she'd fix him a delicious dinner; one of his favorites like chicken merlot then she'd treat him to a massage while he told her all about the last few projects he'd been working on. Then if she wasn't too tired she could wow him with some sexy lingerie and a long awaited session of hot sex.

Driving through Fairmount Park she made her way up the winding roads to their stone tudor style estate in Chestnut Hill. Pulling up to their cobblestone driveway, Hazel noticed another car parked there in front of the house, it was a late model red Toyota coupe. 'Perhaps he has a client or a photo shoot went late' she thought. She knew that more than likely with a car like that it belonged to a model, after all anyone who could afford Ramsey's services usually drove better cars than hers.

Hazel wanted to surprise Ramsey so she carried her bags into the house herself, being extra careful not to make too much noise. By the time he came in from his studio she wanted to at least have their late night dinner started.

Hazel quickly unpacked, freshened up and changed into comfortable shorts and t-shirt. Skipping down to the kitchen to quickly defrost frozen chicken thighs and chop garlic and shallots for her dish. Hazel hummed around her kitchen once again reacquainting herself with everything; when she was away on business Ramsey basically lived like a bachelor and most of her stuff was usually scattered around until she had a chance to reorganize her space again.

By the time she checked the clock and saw that it was already after eleven, she had already poured glasses of merlot for her and Ramsey to enjoy later. Ramsey always said merlot tasted better when it had a chance to breathe. Curious that Ramsey would still be working so late she decided to head out to his studio, perhaps he'd fallen asleep in there. Then she remembered the Toyota in the driveway, from her recollection she never did hear it drive off.

Exiting out the back and walking past their in ground pool, Hazel made her way to Ramsey's art studio way in the rear of their property. She expected to see it flooded with light since Ramsey hated working in dim light, but it wasn't. From what she could see only the flicker of what appeared to be candlelight filtered in through the windows.

Hazel approached feeling suspicious, perhaps the red Toyota belonged to someone other then just a model; or worse perhaps it did belong to a model; one of the many gorgeous women who posed for Ramsey's commercial paintings, ones he would sell on his own without a commissioned client.

Perhaps that car belonged to a pretty young model that for some unknown reason forgot her way home.

Tiptoeing up to the window Hazel saw that her worst suspicion was true. There on the floor of Ramsey's studio was Ramsey and a young woman spread out on a length of canvas. From the looks of her long slender deep chocolate brown body, Hazel assumed she was definitely a model who forgot her way home. She couldn't have been more than twenty two or twenty three tops, Hazel assumed, which was a far cry from her own thirty seven years.

Hazel was fuming, she couldn't believe her eyes; here she had gone out of her way to get home to him early just to find him here getting serviced by young chick. Hazel felt a violent rage building up inside her, as she blindly tried to understand how he could do this to her.

Here she was trying to build a future for them, help them live wealthy beyond their wildest dreams and Ramsey was here getting sucked off by a little Hershey chocolate treat who was at this point filling her mouth with as much of Ramsey's hardness as she could. 'Men are dogs!' She thought, looking at Ramsey who was obviously only thinking with the head he was currently getting sucked off.

It was extremely difficult but she resisted busting in there and breaking up the party. Hazel calculated all her actions, even now with her heart breaking she couldn't make a move without a plan, she needed to get her mind together.

Hazel stood there in the shadows staring and seething, trying to decide what kind of punishment her husband deserved for breaking her trust and her heart the way he was doing right now.

Ramsey, who had no clue that she was standing outside his window, with her fist clenched as tight her jaw, laid casually on his back, facing the girl, his length of jet black locks free and spread around his face like a halo. One of his hands was gripping the paint stained canvas they were lying on and the other was twisted in the girl's head full of natural kinky black hair, very much like she used to wear her own hair back when they first met. His skin the rich color of cedar wood was completely covered in sweat. From sound of his moans Hazel knew he was really enjoying himself, which only made her angrier.

Overcome with emotion, Hazel ran back to the house she needed a moment to decide how she was going to handle Ramsey and his infidelity. Pacing around her kitchen, her mind spun in endless circles unable to make any sense of what was going on.

Hazel Braxton-Taylor was the consummate professional and could negotiate a complicated corporate buy out with no difficulty, but here in her home faced with her husband cheating on her she darted around aimlessly with no idea what do or what to say.

Her first instinct was to find something of his, something he held near and dear to his heart and crush it. Running up to their bedroom, Hazel pulled open every closet door and dresser drawer in their room. Rummaging through his drawer she tried desperately to find something to ruin, something to destroy.

After turning their bedroom inside out, Hazel realized she was acting foolish, destroying Ramsey's things couldn't make up for the fact that he'd cheated on her. Hazel tried to remember who she was, remember that as a businesswoman she was respected, even feared far and wide but none of that mattered right now.

It wasn't till several moments later did she remember he was still outside with that woman, fucking her right there on Hazel's property, on her own estate. "I'm gonna kill him!" she said out loud, her voice cold with determination.

Hazel returned to the kitchen, angrily taking two and three steps at a time on her way day. It occurred to her that she needed to tend to not only Ramsey but also the little tramp that had the nerve to screw her husband right there in her home. Standing now in the kitchen, she glanced at the two glasses of wine and the chef knife she used earlier to chop her vegetables.

Without any further thought she downed both glasses of wine in what felt like one quick gulp, then she grabbed the knife and headed back out to the studio.

By the time she reached the studio again the girl was now straddled over Ramsey riding him. Hazel could see the girls face now and even through her rage had to admit she was more than beautiful. Her features were surprisingly similar to Hazel's own; full lips, high cheekbones, large oval shaped eyes; in fact she could have easily passed for a younger version of Hazel.

Even her body was very similar; the girl sported perky round breast very much like her own c cups, a tiny waist, round curvy hips and long thighs and legs; the only real difference was Hazel was a lighter color of sepia brown and this girl was the deep dark shade of warm earth.

When Hazel approached the window, the girl who was facing the window saw her immediately. Hazel was seconds from barging in with the knife that was gripped tightly in her right hand. What stopped her was the girl, when her gaze met with Hazel's outside the window she smiled and with one hand gestured for Hazel to come to her then held her finger up to her lips telling Hazel to remain quiet as she came.

She did it so sweetly as if she and Hazel were good friends and they were about to share a delicious secret together. The smile on her face was for Hazel unnerving; the look in her eyes were saying 'girl wait to you hear this one'. Though she could not see his face, Ramsey must have had his eyes closed, he didn't appear to have seen her.

Hazel was stunned for the second time tonight, if she expected anything out of a woman who got caught screwing her husband it would be maybe shock, surprise, perhaps her scurrying to cover herself; if nothing else Hazel would have thought she would have at least alerted Ramsey of her presence. This girl did none of those things, she only continued smiling in Hazel direction and gestured to her once more to come inside the studio.

Hazel with the chef knife still gripped in her hand passed through the door, Ramsey caught up in what he was doing failed to notice the warm summer breeze that Hazel brought in with her, the flicker of candlelight as it drank in more oxygen, least of all her standing there at the door. In the heat of the room she drew in the scent of oil paint, candle wax and hot sex, even the scent made her angry and her grip tightened.

The girl still smiling, still gazing directly into Hazel's eyes, began speaking, not to her, but to Ramsey. "Ram, tell me again about your beautiful wife." She said.

"Hazel." Ramsey answered, "You know my wife's name is Hazel."

Hazel stood her palms becoming damp with moisture, her fingers closing even tighter around the knife's handle; wondering what in the hell the girl was doing, what kind of game was she trying to play with her.

"Yeah that's right, beautiful Hazel," the girl said, "Ok, keep your eyes closed and let's pretend again like I was her, what would you be saying to her right now?" The girl asked.

'Pretend again' Hazel heard clearly, did she mean that Ramsey and this woman role-played about her? Hazel was angry and now confused too.

"Damn Angel, I don't know." Ramsey began, "I guess I'd tell her how much I miss her."

"Miss her, or her hot body...you did say her body was hot didn't you" Angel said her eyes locked onto Hazel's gaze.

"Both, yeah her body is hot, but mostly I miss her." Ramsey said honestly, grunting as she moved above.

"What it is about Hazel you miss the most." Angel said her thighs rowing back and forth as she moved still gazing intently into Hazel's eyes.

"Everything, it's kinda like she hasn't been here in years," He said, his breath sounding husky, "even when she does come home…her mind is still at work."

Hazel heard that too but was nonplussed; true Ramsey called her everyday to tell her how much he missed her, but the fact still remained he was here cheating with this young girl, he obviously didn't miss her that much.

She was incensed, and didn't know which bothered her more, his cheating or his having the audacity to discuss her with this woman. Maybe Ramsey missed her, but he certainly wasn't willing to wait one more day for her to return from Hawaii to get his rocks off. She'd been gone this time for only a couple of weeks, what was one more day if he truly cared about being with his wife? Old Ramsey seemed quite happy having his brains screwed out by another woman, a younger more gorgeous woman with glistening ebony skin.

Angel arched her back and curled her body forward against him, gripping her breast and pinching her own nipples as she moved. Though still furious Hazel couldn't help but stare as her husband toes curled up from the passionate ride that that Angel was bestowing upon him.

Never breaking eye contact, Angel's face contorted in a sexy grimace letting Hazel know how good Ramsey was making her feel. Angel's eyes made he look like a hungry animal devouring her prey.

Hazel couldn't remember the last time she herself felt like that but she recognized the expression; Angel was completely and totally being her sexual self, giving herself up to absolute abandon with no restraint. Suddenly she felt a rush of another emotion; she was getting aroused too, and silently cursed herself when her thighs pressed together involuntarily from watching.

Angel's body wriggled and moved like a porn star on fire, if Hazel wasn't so angry, if it wasn't her husband who was being ridden like a horse, Hazel might've even enjoyed the show taking place before her, right there in front of her face. But it wasn't a stranger, it was Ramsey who promised to love, cherish and keep himself only unto her beneath the sexy girl. Still angry her hand held fast to the knife.

"If she were here, who would you rather have ride this big dick of yours, her or me?" Angel asked grinding her hips into him, pumping up and down on him slowly.

"Both!" he said with a laugh, and then sounding more serious said, "Angel, you do feel good up here baby, but to honest can't nobody ride this like Hazel can." Ramsey replied, then as an afterthought said, "well, when she gets around to it."

"Does she make you feel like this?" Angel said and playfully bounced down hard on his erection.

"Mmmm", Ramsey moaned not answering her question, then asked, "Why do you keep bringing up my wife?"

"I dunno, I think it's sexy to hear you say how much you love her, I guess I wish somebody loved me like that." Angel said.

"A lot a good being in love is…she's never here." Ramsey said pulling her body down low on him, sliding inside her harder.

Hazel wanted to shout that she wasn't here because she was working, it's not like she was off having a good time somewhere, definitely not like she was somewhere cheating on him, like he was cheating on her right now.

"Still, I know I'm just a substitute." She said staring into Hazel's eyes from across the room while still grinding her hips into him. "It's Hazel you really want…not me. Look how long I was coming onto you before you even gave me a second look."

"Women come onto me all the time Angel, it comes with my work."

"Soo, what's changed? Why did I finally get a shot at being with the infamous Ramsey Taylor?" She asked never missing a stroke.

"Angel, I'm getting a little tired of waiting for her to hit her damn five million dollar mark just to be important to her again, a man has needs." He said for a moment lying still not responding to Angel's motion. "Guess when she does she'll finally have some time for me and I won't need substitutes anymore." Ramsey said sounding bitter and a little hurt, then "that's if I'm still around."

"Wow, five million…that's a lot of money." Angel said still moving.

"Its just money Angel, there are more important things than money…it's not like either of us would be hurting for cash any day soon." Ramsey answered now beginning to sound angry. "What I'm starting to think is that's just Hazel's excuse not to spend time with me…the next mountain will probably be ten million."

Hazel stood there her mouth dropping open, she was working hard to be successful for the both of them, she thought Ramsey could appreciate that, apparently he didn't. Or perhaps she was being a little selfish, if she had to be honest with herself, Ramsey never really did agree to anything, she just assumed he'd be supportive…he's always been. For the first time since she discovered him cheating, her rage began to subside a bit and her grip on the chef knife began to loosen a little.

"Ram, I'm sure she loves you, she's just ambitious you have to give it to her, I don't think I know any women as successful as your wife." Angel said leaning forward.

"Yeah, her career is important to her, and I love her; that's why I try not to say anything. I just wish I was that important to her too." He laid there still not moving with Angel, though she never stopped, just as she never stopped directly staring into Hazel's now tear filled eyes. Eventually his body began responding again thrusting high up inside Angel causing her to squeal with each of his strokes.

Hazel was feeling something else now, she felt ashamed that she'd left her marriage in the state it was in and jealous that Angel was getting from her husband what she should have been getting.

Ramsey grabbed Angel by the waist lifting himself up higher to match her strokes. "Damn Angel!" He said speeding up his high stroke.

"Don't you want to call me Hazel again?" Angel asked bouncing herself back and forth.

"Naw, that's starting to get old now," Ramsey said slowing down his pace again, sounding sad.

"Mmm, Ram baby don't stop now, I think I'm coming." Angel announced, breaking her gaze from Hazel and shutting her eyes tight. Hazel couldn't believe her ears or her eyes, this girl was about to come right in front of her face; about to remind her how good sex with her husband could be; she herself had almost forgotten.

What this woman was doing took guts; she saw the knife but without fear put Hazel on blast, let her know how royally she had messed up a good marriage. Hazel knew more than anyone that the intensity of her schedule was of her own making, she could have slowed down a long time ago and still been head and shoulder above her competition.

Hazel was more driven today than she'd ever been, from the looks of what was taking place in front of her she succeeded in driving her husband into the arms of another woman as well. After almost fifteen years of marriage she worked harder and longer than she ever had, despite the fact that she was more than ten times wealthier than she was when they'd first started out.

Hazel regarded Angel as her body twisted and she cried out from her orgasm. She still wasn't sure if she wanted kill Angel now or thank her for opening her eyes. She wondered how many times these two had been together, when they got started and why they were so comfortable discussing her marriage between each other.

Then she realized none of that really mattered, what mattered was her husband, the man she loved more than life itself needed to find another woman to give him what she was too busy to give him. She wondered if others like her, men and women had the benefit of seeing what there actions did to their marriage, would it change them, would it make them reevaluate what was truly important in life; for her it did.

Hazel still watching as Angel's body slowed down and shuddered in pleasure understanding that everything that happened in front of her eyes was her fault, Ramsey had reached out to her more times than she could remember. He pleaded with her many times to take some time off, spend a little more time with him, perhaps take a vacation or two and so many times his requests fell on deaf ears. When Hazel got focused, she hyper focused and nothing; not even a loving husband; held any importance at that point.

Angel's trembling slowed completely down, now her hips moved in a slow rhythmic gyration as she raised her eyes to look at Hazel once more. Hazel knew this was a necessary torture; to see where her absence eventually led her husband to, and it pained her to realize she had to see this to finally get Ramsey's point. Hazel's anger was all but gone now, the knife now dangling loosely in her moist hand slipped from her grip and clanked loudly on the stone floor.

"Hazel! Oh Shit!" Ramsey said startled and stunned, moving from beneath Angel, jumping up from the floor nearly knocking Angel over on her head in the process.

Hazel looked at her husband's body, as he stood across the room naked and still aroused; he was wet, drenched with sweat and magnificent. His arms, were definitely the arms of an artist she'd almost forgotten how sculpted they were, his thighs and calves were still well defined and the hard on he was still sporting was for lack of a better word incredible.

But what struck her more than anything was the look in his eyes; she wondered how long the sadness had been there, how long he'd carried around that look of loneliness.

The man standing before her looking scared out of his mind knew her more than she knew herself. He loved her long before the business world had ever heard of her, even back when the only ride she could afford was her own late model Toyota coupe.

Hazel realized her priorities had been off, sure she cared about he career, but her marriage should have been her first concern; what good was a five million dollar net worth if it was going to cost her the man she loved. How much longer would he have played this game with women like Angel, how much longer would it have been before he completely gave up on her and moved on.

At this point Angel was wrapping herself up, tucking in her towel she said directly to Hazel, "I'm really sorry Hazel."

Hazel approached her and stood face to face with Angel and looked carefully at the woman who in the strangest way just helped her save her marriage, the scent from her own husband still rising up from Angel's skin and said, "No you're not and neither am I." and then finally returning Angel's smile said, "thank you."

Ramsey stood there not know what was going on as far as he knew Hazel had just walked in on him screwing one of his young models, he had no idea she'd been standing there for several minutes. "Hazel I...I...I." He stammered out.

"You what Ramsey, love me?" Hazel said while approaching her husband. With each step she took she casually removed a piece of her own clothing so that by the time she was standing before her husband every piece of her clothes were shed.

The two of them stood there for what seemed like an endless moment while Ramsey cleared his mind of the shock of Hazel catching him in the act of cheating, and without killing him at first sight. Looking into her eyes he saw understanding there and forgiveness and it gave him enough courage to respond. "Yes Hazel, I love you."

Hazel let him pull her into his arms and kiss her on the lips. His mouth tasted of Angel, his skin smelled of her. Hazel drew in that scent and recorded it to memory; it was her penance for ignoring her husband for so long.

Angel looked at both of them with a satisfied look on her face while climbing back into her clothes. Before making her way out the door, she paused to watch them once more, Hazel had taken her rightful place on the canvas next to her husband who was now holding her tightly, caressing her skin and covering her face with passionate kisses. Angel started to tell Ramsey goodbye, let him know she would never return, but she knew she didn't have to. After tonight she was certain that Hazel was going to make sure that Ramsey never needed another substitute ever again.

Train Ride

Eva was running late again, she'd missed her eight eleven train that took her into Center City. Now she impatiently waited at Fernrock Station for the eight twenty two tapping her black Donna Karan pumps against the concrete platform; even with her proud stance and wearing stiletto pumps she was still barely a few inches above five feet.

Pacing back and forth Eva's pretty brown face twisted in frustration, wishing for some miracle that would make the train come a little earlier. The soft morning breeze blowing through the bouncy layers of her thick dark hair and against her cocoa brown skin couldn't calm her; the sound of early summer birds chirping did nothing to relieve her anxiety.

She must have peered down the tracks a dozen times though as usual the train didn't come until it was supposed to. Lately she'd been late every Monday, it was starting to become a really bad habit of hers.

She hated catching the eight twenty two, no only did it make her late but that train was always so crowded, she'd have to fight to get a seat. Today, though, she was in luck, when the doors opened and the passenger piled in she was able to catch the last seat by the door before the doors closed.

Once the conductor announced it was the Express Train on the Orange Broad Street Line and the next stop would Olney Avenue the doors closed and the train began moving. Eva ran through her mind the last few Monday lateness excuses she'd told her boss Rob. She'd gone through as many as she could possibly think of and though his expression was really kind and understanding, she could see on his face that Rob was starting to get fed up with her excuses. One more and she would be written up, he more than sternly told her so; that would be the first step to getting terminated, her job was pretty strict on attendance. She was sure that pretty soon he was going to pull her into his office to discuss it.

Eva decided just to tell him the truth; she just didn't want to get out of bed this morning. 'Whatever happened, happened', she thought, though truth be told she was scared silly that she might lose her job.

Besides, Rob could read through a lie with no problem and his skeptical looks just left her feeling uneasy the rest of the day. She felt really bad lying to him, Rob was such a nice guy; he could be a lot harder on her than he chose to be.

The train pulled into Olney station; Eva groaned when she saw the all the people waiting to get on the train. Each of them packed on like sardines squeezing in tighter and tighter.

Eva just sat there clutching her handbag and her little tote that contained her lunch, and a new pair of panty hose still in the pack. She absolutely hated wearing them, but her ancient director Sue still insisted all of the women wore them during working hours. Rushing out of her door this morning, she decided to wait till she got to her office to put them on.

Right before the door closed an elderly woman walked up towards the door, someone shouted to the conductor to wait; usually they would pull off anyway, but this conductor was kind enough to wait. She got on the train, slowly;

managing with some difficulty to get herself, her walking stick and her bag on before the doors closed again.

There was very little space on the train, so little that the old woman couldn't even find a bar low enough for her to hold on to. Eva realized her seat was the closest for the woman to get to before the train started moving so she offered her, her seat. "Bless your heart," the older woman said as Eva helped guide her into the seat.

"You're welcome Mam,'" Eva said with a smile reaching high above to hold onto one of the overhead bars.

By the next stop the old woman was ready to get off the train, but before Eva could reclaim her seat another woman, this one not nearly as old plopped herself heavily into the seat.

Eva just sighed and continued holding the bar, the woman not missing but ignoring the roll of Eva's eyes as she made herself comfortable in the seat.

The next two stops went about the same; too many people getting on and too few getting off making it more uncomfortable than ever. By the time the train pulled out of Spring Garden station there was barely enough bar space for Eva to hold onto.

When the train started again, it did so with a jolt, harder than usual. The motor grinded loudly before pulling out slowly, Eva moaned when the train didn't pick up much speed. 'Great' she thought, 'I'm gonna be even later than I thought.'

Just as the train pulled past the Race and Vine station, it groaned again jolting even harder than before, forcing many of the passengers to bump soundly into each other. Suddenly there was a surge of power, the lights for several second shone ten times brighter than before, and then everything went dark.

The passengers reacted immediately in a panic the sound of their shouting was almost deafening. People tried using their cell phones in vain; there was no cellular service whatsoever there inside the subway tunnel. Eva held her bags closely to her body afraid that thieves and pickpockets would start having a field day on the darkened train.

It wasn't long before the conductor's voice came on over a scratchy emergency PA system asking everyone to remain calm assuring them that everything would be fine and they'd be on their way as soon as possible. That seemed to quiet the passengers for a while and Eva was happy to know someone was working on whatever the problem was.

Eva sensed some movement behind her, peering into the darkness trying to make out the form standing near her. "Eva?" a voice said over the noise.

"Who are you?" Eva said not sure whether to panic or be glad that someone recognized her.

"Late again, huh?"

"Rob?" She said recognizing her boss' voice behind her. Rob stood maybe six inches taller than her even in her high heels, and about twice her width in frame. Rob was what some would call a gentle giant. In the darkness she tried to picture his face, she assumed he was smiling; Rob rarely had an angry expression unless he was under extreme pressure at work; usually brought on by his superior director Sue.

"Yeah, guess I'm late today too." He said with a chuckle. Rob didn't have classically handsome features, skin the shade of chocolate milk, ordinary hair, cut into a ordinary style, warm brown eyes that looked either like he was being understanding or perhaps just sleepy.

His clothes were standard office issue; dark pants, light shirt and a striped tie. Eva imagined he probably shopped at a regular men's clothing outlet. If she could think of a word that best described him she would most likely say he was 'steady'.

That however, was ok to Eva, who in her twenty-eight years she had dated some exceptionally fine men who turned out to be exceptional flops. She was beginning to appreciate other qualities about a man; which had nothing to do with how fine he was or what kind of car he drove.

But as for her boss Rob, most would say he was pretty average, nothing to write home about; but there was something about him, something that only a woman could sense that made him kinda sexy. At least Eva thought so.

"At least I'm not alone on this train, I'm just waiting for something crazy to break out." Eva said sounding genuinely worried, stuck on a blacked out subway train under Center City wasn't her idea of the safest and secure situation.

"Don't worry, I'll look out for you." Rob replied, his words making her feel safe despite the potential for chaos on a crowded train.

"It's hot as hell in here yo! I got claustrophobia! It's probably those fucking terrorist again yo!" a passenger from the other end of the car shouted, the faceless voice rousing up the rest of train again, the volume once again beginning to rise.

"It's one in every crowd." Eva said to Rob disgusted, imagining what kind of frenzy the wrong ignorant comment could rile up. True it was starting to get warmer on the train, but nothing unbearable.

"Yeah well, as long as we remain sharp, we'll be ok." He said

"Coming through! Please be Patient! We'll be up and running momentarily!" Yelled the voice of someone at the other end of the car, Eva saw several flashlight beams as a crew of men made their way through the crowd of people.

When they made it past Eva and Rob, Rob had to move out of their way causing him to press even tighter against Eva's backside. To avoid knocking her over, Rob wrapped one arm around Eva's waist to keep them steady. Even after they past Rob still held onto her tightly until he realized what he'd been doing, "Oh, Eva…I'm sorry." Rob said trying his best to separate his body from hers the best he could.

It was really no use; they were packed in there like sardines. Eva could hear the embarrassment in his voice, "It's ok Rob, really." She said, "I'm just grateful you're here." What Eva didn't say was how good it felt to feel her little body pressed against such a big solid man.

Outside the window, in the distance, she could see on the track right next to the one the train she was in sat on what looked like emergency lights, flashing red and white coming closer to the train. "Looks like help is on its way," Rob said.

"Thank God." Eva said, peering into the darkness trying to figure out what the men with the flashlights were doing. It didn't occur to her till several moments later that Rob was still straining not to press himself against her butt, she could only imagine how uncomfortable he was. "Relax Rob, you're not bothering me."

"I just didn't want you to think…" He said still sounding embarrassed.

Eva shifted her body around now facing Rob, hoping that would ease some of his discomfort, "Is that better?" She said hoping he could see her smiling in the darkness.

"Umm, I guess" Rob said his chest now pressed against her round breast, then a few seconds later he said, "Your perfume Eva, you smell really pretty."

"Thanks Rob, I just bought it. It's called Pink." Eva had just made a trip to Victoria Secrets that Saturday and among her purchases was the sweet floral scented perfume.

"I really like it." Rob said.

Eva let herself sniff at Rob's chest trying to see if she could detect the scent of any cologne on him and she couldn't, Rob just smelled freshly washed, clean. He probably didn't even own a bottle of cologne. Eva wondered when his birthday was; perhaps she'd buy a nice bottle or two for him then.

The two stood there close enough to slow dance, not really saying much, while other voices and conversations buzzed all around them. Ten minutes had passed and though people were getting antsy everyone seemed to remain patient, people had fallen into chitchat with whoever sat next to them, and most of the conversations were about everyone being late for work.

Eva thought about Rob, she knew he was about thirty-four years old and had never been married; he had his own house in Mt. Airy and drove a new Chrysler. Like many people Rob took the train to save on parking since it was so expensive in Center City.

Rob had one child a preteen daughter, Alyssa who lived with her mother in another state, and he proudly had one of every school picture she'd ever taken all around his office. Besides that though, Eva didn't know much else about the man with the starched cotton shirt and business tie in front of her.

Rob for the most part was quiet, so quiet that Eva wondered what he was thinking. She really didn't have to wonder for long. Just about where her belly was Eva could feel stiffening in his pants and as much as he tried to angle himself away from her, she could definitely feel it rising. "Rob…are you?" She asked.

"I'm so sorry, Eva…" He stammered out like an embarrassed schoolboy.

Eva regarded him in the warm darkness, amazed at how bashful a man who managed dozen of people on a daily basis was in a one on one situation like they were in now; Eva found it charming.

The fact they he was getting turned on by her wasn't exactly a bad thing either, especially since her own body had responded to his erection so strongly, her nipples were beginning to tense beneath her blouse, her palms, armpits and between her thighs were becoming warm and moist as well. It told her if nothing else there was definitely an animal attraction going on between the two of them.

Eva figured she could handle this in one of two ways, either say something flip that could make him feel even more embarrassed or let him know she was feeling him just as much as he was apparently feeling her; she decided on the latter. Eva leaned her body closer to his moving slightly against his erection. "Don't be sorry Rob…it's fine, really," she said.

"You sure?" He said leaning towards her enjoying the feel of her hips moving against him.

"Mmm Hmm," she said quietly feeling herself getting turned on too, "you like me Rob?" she asked still moving her hips as much as their confinement would allow.

"Yeah, I do." Rob said without hesitation, his deep voice sounding husky.

"For how long?" Eva asked.

"Since I first met you." He replied.

She thought about that, Eva had been on her job, close to four years now and in all these years Rob never let on that he was anything more than a good manager to her and many times when her pretty boy boyfriends were acting up; an excellent listener as well. "Why didn't you say anything?" She asked.

"I'm your boss." He replied, his voice sounding sensual as he whispered.

It was strange to hear him sounding like that and of all places on a broken down crowded train, but Eva liked it, and she liked him. She began wondering what a big man like him would be like in bed how it would feel riding him, to have that thickness sliding in and out of her. Eva was pretty aggressive sexually, she wondered if Rob could appreciate that, something told her he could.

"You know, I like you too." She said her hand raising up to stroke the outline in his pants. The hardness there grew with each stroke of her hand.

"Why didn't you say anything?" He asked.

"'Cause…you're my boss." She said coyly. She wanted him to know she was just as turned on as he was, so to make her point she took his hand and slid it up her skirt letting his big fingers rest against her panty.

Without hesitating Rob slipped two fingers beneath the fabric and allowed his fingertips to trace her heart shaped bikini trim, before sliding a finger lower and toying with her lips there.

Eva was on fire, in the crowded loudness of the hot train her boss was silently getting her off. She began grinding her hips against his hand, rotating them in little concentrated circles. All the while she was still stroking his hardness through the fabric of his pants.

Rob slipped his other arm around Eva and drew her in close, moving his shoulders down low enough to gain better access, he dipped his finger in deeper while holding her body tightly against his. Eva felt him in her hand, rigid and ready for her. Being on the train was the only thing that stopped her from falling to her knees and taking him in her mouth.

Eva lifted herself up on her toes, opening her legs as wide as they could go with the other people pressing in against her, dropping her hips down in a tight little rhythm against his hands.

Eva was close, seconds close to letting go all over his hands. 'What a crazy morning', she thought. She was more excited at this very second than she'd even been. Here on a train of dozens of hot, fussing people, her boss of all people was about to make her come.

Then she did come and all at once every other body except theirs seemed to disappear around her. Eva barely heard the train crew calling out eta's to the passengers letting them know the train was sure to be up and running very soon and offering the telephone number to the lateness excuse line should their employers need verification. Closing her eyes tightly, Eva let herself succumb to the feeling that was making her knees weak. Eva forgot about being late for work, the people on the train, even the train…everything.

In her mind she could hear Janet singing softly, "Anytime…or any place, I don't care whose around." And she didn't care, she didn't care if anyone noticed when her breath drew in sharply from his touch, she didn't care if anyone could above the noise hear her moaning softly into Rob's chest. The only thing that held fast in her mind that moment was Rob, the hardness that seemed to still be growing in his pants and his fingers that were making her tremble silently as she came.

146

Still holding her closely, Rob slowly removed his right hand from between her legs and joined it to his left, latching his fingers together tightly around her waist, without a word Rob bent down and kissed her wholly on her mouth.

Eva opened her mouth wide and let Rob's tongue travel over hers getting more excited as he sucked on her full bottom lip. Savoring the feel of his lips on hers Eva wondered what was next for them. Was Rob going to take things back to status quo, would they just be boss and employee or would there be a repeat of this morning once more but under more pleasant circumstances?

Still wondering and while still in his embrace the train made a loud whooshing sound as the air conditioning started and the lights came back on. The other riders shouted and applauded as the train began moving again. Only Eva wished it the train was dark and still as it had been before.

The bright light brought her back to reality as did Rob removing his arms from around her waist, now standing very close still but at a respectable distance from her.

The woman in front of her, the one who had stolen her seat stared up at Eva with and evil scowl on her face. She was probably the only person who realized what had happened between Rob and Eva. "Don't hate!" Eva mouthed to her, and then with a toss of her hair and roll of her eyes, Eva turned her back to the woman.

Daring to look up into his eye Eva saw what she hoped would be there, Rob was smiling at her his eyes gently letting her know they'd crossed a line that was for now going to have to remain crossed. Rob wasn't nearly done with her yet. "Think we can continue this later?" Rob asked.

"Definitely." She answered.

Finally, reaching the City Hall stop of the subway both of them rushed up into the underground concourse to the basement level of their building. Normally Eva would take the spiral stairs that led up to the corner courtyard and the famous giant clothespin statue directly across from City Hall and grab a news paper and orange juice from the vendor on the corner, but today she was way too late for that.

Once on the elevator, both of them allowed themselves a second to catch their breath. Checking his watch Rob said, "You know were both over a half hour late."

"I know," Eva said worriedly. "But you're never late Rob, this is like my tenth lateness.

"Eleventh," Rob corrected her. "Guess, I'll have to meet with you sometime this morning to discuss your attendance," Rob said flashing her a grin.

"I guess you will," Eva replied getting off at her floor. Looking back at Rob she saw he was still watching her intently and decided to throw a little extra twist in her walk as she made her way down the hallway to her desk.

By eleven thirty Eva was close to catching up on her work, her morning had been so busy since she arrived she didn't really have a moment to think about Rob and all that had taken place on the train, not until he was standing over her desk with what looked liked an attendance write up.

"Eva," he said sounding stern with a serious look on his face, "what time did you get this morning?"

Her co-workers all stopped what they were doing, and listened with concern. Eva was just about to answer in a flippant tone that Rob knew exactly what time she'd gotten in since he was just as late as she was, but stopped short when she saw the gleam in his eyes. Rob was playing up his managerial role for the others, all she had to do was go along with it. Without giving it away to everyone else that he wanted her, Rob let Eva know what was on his mind when he raised his index and middle finger to his nose and inhaled deeply.

"Umm, I'm sorry Rob," she said clearing her throat and trying her best to sound sincere, "the train I rode in on, broke down around Race and Vine. We were stuck under ground for a good while. I was a half hour late, but I have this number you can call to verify it."

"Mmm hmm, I heard about that train Rob," Her co-worker Sandy said taking Eva's defense. "My sister was on that train and she didn't get to work till after 9:30."

Rob looked thoughtful for a minute, making a quick note on the notepad he was carrying then said before walking away, "very well, but I'll still need you to bring that number to me Eva."

"Ok Rob, I'll be up in a minute." Eva called after him as he exited the department, squeezing her legs together, trying not to show how excited she was.

Eva waited long enough not to be obvious before she dashed away to the elevator to join Rob in his office. On the elevator ride up to his floor Eva felt herself anticipating Rob's touch, wondering how far they were going to take it now that they were in the office.

Arriving at his office door, Eva tapped twice before Rob called out, "Come in." Once inside he mouthed, "lock the door", quietly so that his boss Sue, whose office was across the hall could not hear.

"I have that number for you Rob." Eva said with a smile on her face approaching his desk. Eva had been in Rob's office dozen of times before; more than anything to discuss her lateness; it looked the same as always with his company awards, motivational wall art, some of his football trophies from college and pictures of his pretty daughter; but this time was different, after what transpired in the darkness of the train, everything would now be different with him.

Rob sat back in his leather chair eyeing her from behind his desk, his expression not easily readable. "Eva, I want you to know, I really like you, I'm mean what happened this morning was great, but I don't want you to think I'm taking advantage of you, me being your boss and all…I…" Sounding unsure, his mind grappling with the situation.

Eva waited several seconds for him to finish his sentence and when he didn't she began feeling impatient. 'Unh, uh…you're not gonna lose your nerve now', she thought. Eva realized she was going to have to take charge when it came to Rob, to everyone else he was the big boss, but to her he was her new teddy bear. "So you're my boss…" She said matter of factly.

Rob looked at her, the wanting obvious in his eyes, not taking his eyes off her body he said, "There's a lot to consider here…"

Eva wanting to pick up right where left off at on the train, all this talking could wait. Eva decided to make the first move. "Sit up in your chair Rob," she said in a voice that made Rob immediately sit up.

"Ok." Rob answered humored by her tone.

"Listen baby, you like me and I like you, that's all that matters," she said walking around to his desk switching her hips as she moved. Eva stopped only long enough to slip out of her panties and skirt, keeping on her top and her Donna Karan pumps. Pushing his keyboard and paperwork aside, she hoisted her petite body up on his desk, plopping her bare ass on his desk, spreading her legs apart, her feet dangling in front of him. "Now, you were saying on the train?"

"I was saying…" Rob said slowly, staring at her heart shaped trim, "I really want to finish what we started." Rob answered smiling.

"Uh huh, me too Rob, so stand up." Eva said and as he stood she removed her blouse then her bra.

Rob without hesitation took both of her breast into his hands and began caressing her nipples. "Damn, Eva," he said below his breath taking in her nude body, before taking one nipple between his lips.

"Mmm, that's right." Eva moaned, careful to keep her tone low so as not to alert Sue. While Rob entertained himself with her breast, she reached her hand down to his belt and unfastened his belt, then his zipper. Feeling him skin on skin, Eva sized Rob up in her hands and was satisfied with what she felt. 'I can work with that.' She thought to herself, while stroking him in her hands.

"Now sit back down Rob," Eva commanded. As he did his pants fell down around his ankles displaying thick masculine thighs and legs. 'Powerhouse' she thought to herself, seeing that her big man was made of quite a bit of muscle; Eva was suddenly turned on even more.

Seated now again in his leather chair, Eva slid off his desk and first dropping to the floor filled her mouth with Rob, making him stiffer and stiffer as she licked and sucked.

Eva barely wanted to pull her mouth away, the taste of him between her lips intoxicating her; but she knew what kind of time they were working with, pretty soon her co-workers would wonder what was taking her so long, at any time someone could knock at Rob's door and force them to end their interlude. With that in mind, Eva rose to her knees and after turning him in his chair around to face the view of City Hall, she climbed into his lap and rode him with her back facing him.

Grasping the arms of his chair, Eva moved her hips back against him, throwing her ass and hips hard against his lap. Rob first responded like he didn't know what hit him but the more she moved against him, the more he picked up on her rhythm. Before either of them knew what was happening, they were coming in succession; first Eva and seconds later Rob came with a grunt then a deep groan, a growl almost.

"Shit Eva!" Rob said wiping his brow while trying to compose himself.

"There's more where that came from Rob." Eva said still in her heels slipping back into her bra, blouse and skirt.

"Eva I want all of you, not just a quickie." Rob replied, his eyes looking puppy dog lost.

"And you will baby…you will. Like I said before I like you Rob, I like you a lot. You're more to me than just my boss." Eva said feeling sexy and powerful, in just a few minutes she could tell she'd practically blown Rob's mind.

"When will I see you again?" Rob said, finally getting up to fix his clothes and straighten his tie.

Eva wanted to hug him, who knew just from one shot he'd turn to putty like that. Eva realized she had to be careful with a man like Rob, he wasn't one of her ex-boyfriends, he was sweet sensitive and caring…almost naive; she made up her mind right there to be sure to treat him with kindness and respect at all times.

Bending down to the floor she picked up her panties, they were a brand new pair of Victoria Secrets'. Walking back around Rob's desk she slid the pair in his left hand and folded it close and said, "hold onto these for me Rob…something tells me I'll need to pick em up at your place tonight."

"Is that right?" Rob asked looking genuinely happy to hear the news.

"Yeah...that's right." Eva said with a smile, 'if Rob thought this was something, wait till he see what I can do with silk scarves and a bed,' she thought.

"Whew, I can't wait for that." Rob said as Eva turned to walk out the office. "Oh Eva," Rob said, his voice returning to his usually managerial tone."

"Yes baby?" Eva said turning to face him again with a smile on her face, knowing he wasn't ready this soon for round two.

Straightening his tie and reaching for the pile of papers that Eva had shifted over on his desk. After a quick search he seemed to find what it was that he was looking for; it was the papers he had in his hand when he came down to her desk. "There's still the matter of your excessive lateness Eva...I'm afraid I'm going to have to write you up."

Therapy

I was freezing by the time I reached Dr. Jeffery Solomon's office, after all it took me a train and two busses just to get all the way out here in Overbrook Park from where I lived in Frankford, and a cold, rainy November in Philly is no time to be taking public transportation; but I had no choice my car broke down yesterday and I had scheduled this appointment months ago, so there was no way I was going to miss it.

Val told me about Dr. Solomon, she suggested back in the summer that I get in to see him as soon as I possible could. "Make you an appointment now girl and you might get seen by Christmas," she said, "but believe you me, it will definitely be worth the wait."

'And the cost too', I was thinking because Dr. Solomon was expensive and he didn't take insurance. Walking into his office I was directed by a receptionist to take a seat. While waiting, I checked my purse once again to make sure the two hundred and fifty dollars I'd saved up was there, and yeah it was there snuggled between my appointment card and my Transpass, though I knew it was there I would just hate to have come all this way and not be able to be seen.

When Val first told me she was seeking therapy, I thought she was crazy to even consider it, no matter how bad things got me thought, "It couldn't be that bad", and I told her that too... but she said this doctor that her boss referred her to specialized in helping female patients who for whatever reason had fallen into a slump. For Val it was her divorce from Paul and that messy old custody battle that had her in a funk.

But sure enough just after a few sessions with Dr. Solomon, old Val was back to herself again, actually better. Everything about her seemed to improve, her appearance, her outlook on life…everything. The difference in her was so drastic; it was like she had gone on Extreme Makeover or something.

Whenever I asked her what he did that made such a big difference, she'd just say I had to experience it for myself. Truth be told I want some of that in my life, I mean I haven't been though a divorce or anything, but for me well it's combination of things that was getting to me like my boring marriage to Eric, our jacked up credit situation, the ghetto neighborhood that after thirteen years we still lived in, my hooptie car that breaks down on a regular and takes me weeks to get up and running again, and so on. Lately, I've been getting so depressed that, I'll just sit and a dark room and cry for hours until I feel better…and that ain't me.

If there was anyway that Dr. Solomon could help me, I was willing to pay for it. I thought as I sat shivering in his office sipping on the hot tea the receptionist made for me. Once I was sufficiently warm, she had me fill out some paperwork while I waited for my appointment, which was mostly a questionnaire. When I got down to question number fourteen 'what was the date of your last period?' it struck me odd that a therapist would need to know that; but then again, a lot of the questions on the form struck me as odd; but I figured these people know what they were doing and went ahead and answered them.

When I was finished I handed my paperwork back to the receptionist. Leaning my head in past her little glass window,

I said "Excuse me, but um, how long does my session last?" Wondering how much counseling I would get for my two hundred and fifty.

"Normally two hours, but since this is your first session, it may take a little longer, depends on how deep the session goes." The receptionist replied in a crisp business like voice.

"Oh ok," I said, thinking that wasn't half bad, here I thought I was getting the standard 'one hour and your own your way' treatment. But two hours 'wow', I could probably get a lot off of my chest in that much time.

Before long the doctor opened his office door and invited me in. He was a brother, which shouldn't have surprised me; I just didn't expect it; and a pretty good looking one too. Dr. Solomon stood about six feet three, six feet four maybe. He was tall, built long like he ran ball. His skin was dark, his face clean shaven, his hair neatly cut, and with a pair of black reading glasses perched on his nose making him look very doctor-ish. Along with that he was dressed "business casual" in a rose colored oxford shirt, gray slacks and black shoes.

Walking into his office I felt almost at home, there was no desk, just a leather sofa, loveseat and chair around a marble coffee table all of it seated nicely on top of a tasteful area rug. The light in his office was soft, casting gentle shadows in the corners. There were rows and rows of books, photos and pieces of art on his shelves. On another wall there was a flat plasma screen television and some more wall art hung around it. The room smelled faintly like sandalwood and jasmine and there was something smooth and jazzy playing softly from a sound system somewhere. The room looked more like the living room of a well laid out bachelor pad than a therapist office. 'Cozy' I thought as the doctor offered me a beverage; which I declined, before taking a seat next to me.

"So Miss Jones…what brings you here today?" Dr. Solomon said, sitting closer to me than I thought he should.

"Are you a real doctor?" I blurted out, half because I wanted to know and half because I was too nervous to just jump in and start rattling off my problems.

"Yes, I'm a certified alternative healer," he said, then "But my guess is that question was not what brought you here today."

My eyes dropped down, yeah he was right but how do you start off with "my life is one big boring mess" it just doesn't roll off the tongue that well. I didn't expect to get nervous, but here the nerves were starting to jump around and do tumblesaults in my belly.

Taking a deep breath, I tried focusing on something else, like his hands. The nails were neatly trimmed, clean and buffed nicely. 'Nice, he gets manicures,' I thought. "No I guess that's not why I'm here." I said still not looking him in his eyes. I let my eyes wander to his feet, no bigger than average, maybe a size eleven or twelve; so if the myth was true he'd be nothing to brag about.

"Then why are you here?" He asked intently, ok now I was looking in his eyes and they were pretty, clear, deep and a warm brown and I realized this close I could smell him, just barely, he was wearing something Givenchy, I couldn't put my finger on which one it was though.

"I'm miserable and I want to know why." That's not what I meant, I chewed down on my tongue a little, I hate when I say things the wrong way, and I always do that. "What I mean is, I used to be happy...I want to feel like that again." There that's what I meant; the second time was always a charm.

"Mmm okay". He said as though he was considering something, and then asked "what's making you feel that way?'

"Everything!" I blurted out now knowing why I was feeling so frustrated. I guess I didn't want to have to go into details about my problems, but there was no other way.

"Your tense, Miss Jones...before we can proceed we are going to have to get you to relax a little."

"You can call me Donna," I said nodding. He was right, my muscles were in tangled up knots.

"Turn around Donna." Dr. Solomon said matter of factly.

"What?" I wasn't sure what he meant.

"With your back facing me, turn and look towards the television." With that he picked up a remote and flicked on the plasma screen. On popped a recording of a calm seascape and then some seconds later the images changed to an even calmer view of wind blowing through the forest rustling the leaves.

"Oh that's nice." I said watching as the images changes from one calming scene to another.

"I'd like try something before we proceed, would that be okay?" The doctor said his voice sounding mellow in my ear.

"Yeah, that would be okay." I said enjoying the view, it was like looking out of the window but every so often your surroundings changed on you.

Placing two hands on me he began expertly kneading my shoulders, when I felt the knots loosen and melt away he nodded in approval, "That's right Donna relax, there's no rush here we'll take all the time you need." He said leaning in almost whispering in my ear.

His hands were incredible, I felt like I was being transported when he touched me, now I'd never been to therapy before so I was assuming it was supposed to be like this at least I was hoping, and if it was I was coming to therapy more often.

"Alright Donna", he said still kneading, take a few deep breaths and tell me what's been bothering you."

"OK, where do I start…I feel like I'm stuck in a rut and I have no clue how to get out of it." The words poured from my mouth like water as he continued rubbing.

"Go on."

"My marriage has been a joke, I guess I gotta admit myself the only reason we got married in the first place was because I was pregnant with little Eric. Even at that we used to have fun together, but not anymore. Now all he does is work, play video games and watch football while I do everything else." I said the thoughts just flowing.

"Ok, What I hear you saying is you're not satisfied with the direction your marriage has taken…is that correct?" Dr. Solomon asked.

"Yeah, that's it exactly, you get married and think 'wow this is going to be great me and him forever'. Then forever happens and your pissed the hell off!"

To my surprise, Dr. Solomon chuckled, now I was sure your therapist wasn't supposed to laugh at you.

"You laughing?" I asked feeling my shoulders start to tense up again.

"No, no" he said, "I don't find your situation humorous at all, if anything your delivery is funny, but forgive me, laughing was not appropriate."

I considered his apology, and true people tell me that way I say things sometimes come off as a little comical, I'd heard that dozens of times before. "Mmm, it's okay doc, I tend to make a joke out of everything, even when I'm crying."

"Hmm, sounds like you already have way of handling your stress." Then walking around to face me asked, "Or is it a way to mask it?"

"I dunno, maybe it's just easier to deal with." I said looking at the changing pictures on the screen; right now they were easier to look at then him.

"Ok, that's fair, now tell about this rut you find yourself in, what do you think would help take you out of it?"

"I was hoping you'd tell me that." I said looking at him, and then I asked, "what was it that got Val out of her rut?"

"Val?" He asked, then looking at my chart said, "Oh yes, Valerie Dugan," he said nodding, "she referred you to me?"

"Yup, she said you helped her out when that awful divorce she went through almost took her six feet under." I said.

"Well…" Dr. Solomon said, "Without discussing details about another patient let me just say that some of my patients life experiences have made them; how should I say; forget that they are beautiful, strong, vibrant, sensual women. Oftentimes my assistance helps them get back on track."

That was a lot to take in, and I understood most of it, but I needed him to break it down in English exactly what he planned to do for me. "You say all that to mean what Doc?"

"That with your cooperation, I can help you unleash the real you, the true you…once she's freed from the confines of what's affecting her, once we tap into the woman you were meant to be, you'll find that any and all obstacles your find yourself facing in life you will easily be able to overcome."

"Overcome a bad marriage, bad credit and living in a bad neighborhood, all from tapping into something inside of me…yeah right!" I looked at the doctor like he'd gone crazy, if there were something in me that could change all that, wouldn't I have done it by now? I felt like he was trying sell me a load of shit and I wasn't buying.

"It's true, but like I said, only with your cooperation…your full cooperation." Dr Solomon said looking at me.

His gaze was unnerving; he looked at me like he held the golden ticket to happiness and I thought 'it couldn't be that easy', but then I thought about Val and how after just her few first sessions she was acting different, even dressing different; a good different and I wanted to be that was too. "What do I need to do?" I asked.

'First I'd like you to lie back on the couch, if it makes you more comfortable you can remove your shoes if you'd like." The doctor said.

I decided to take his advice and slipped my shoes off my feet and then laid back on his couch. The leather was butter soft and molded to body easily; I was comfortable in seconds.

"Ok now I want you to close your eyes and breath deeply along with me." As he counted off several times I began to inhale with him and exhale with him real slow and deep.

"Good." He said, "Now I want you to reach into your past and pull up certain memories, once you find them I want you to hold onto them, keep them at the surface. We'll need these feelings to remain fresh if were to unlock the deepest part of you."

Then the doctor had me dig into my memory and recall moments when I felt my most beautiful; I said my prom and my wedding day. He had me describe what made me feel beautiful on those days and told me again to hold onto those memories.

Then he asked at what time did I feel my strongest; I told him when I gave birth to little Eric because I was in labor for over twenty-four hours and when my Dad died 'cause on the day of his funeral, I felt like I had to hold up the whole family that day.

Again he told me to hold onto that memory; I was starting to feel like there was too much going on in my head; my prom dress, my wedding veil, seeing baby Eric for the first time, holding my mother up when she almost collapsed in front of my Dad's closed coffin. I was started to doubt if this man could do anything for me other than make me feel uneasy.

Then he said, "Now tell me when you've felt your sexiest, most sensual self."

And I drew a blank, I mean I knew I was somewhat attractive, I know my ass looked good in a pair of jeans, but sexy and sensual? I couldn't really remember.

"Dig deep Donna, when was the last time you were purely and completely a sensual and erotic creature? Tell me when if you need me to help you."

"When I was…um. When I did…" Hell I didn't know; I was mother, a wife, a daughter and a data entry clerk. Outside of that I didn't think about myself that much, trying now was starting to make me feel uncomfortable.

"Donna, let me know if you need my help." Dr. Solomon said once again.

I struggled for several moments longer, embarrassed that I couldn't easily answer such a basic question. "What does that have to do with anything?" I asked getting annoyed.

"Well, you not answering tell me that this is the area in your life that we need to work on. You need to know your sexy, worthy of feeling that way, being that way and living that way." Then, "Donna, I can think your special, amazing, strong, sexy, sensual...whatever. It's not until you think it that we can help make a difference in your life."

'Sexy and sensual', those were two words that I did not equate with myself ever. Halle Berry was sexy maybe, Beyonce was sensual, but me...I was just plain old ordinary Donna from Frankford, just miserable Donna, who was stuck in her ordinary miserable life. Just then I knew I wanted to feel something more, I wanted to somehow identify with something greater than just ordinary. Before I lost my nerve and right before I felt my throat beginning to tighten and tears build beneath my closed eyelids I heard myself whisper, "help me."

"Are you sure?" The doctor asked.

With my eyes still closed, I cleared my throat and said this time a little louder, "Yes I'm sure...I want you to help me."

"Ok then", he replied making his way around to the couch, I could hear his footsteps as they brushed across the carpet and the fine hairs on my arms stood up to the sound. When he sat down at the end of the sofa a chill ran down my spine. I knew something was about to happen, I didn't know what; but I knew it was something.

"First, Dr. Solomon said, I need two things from you."

"What?" I asked ready to give anything.

"Your understanding that I'm a professional and what transpires from this point on is purely part of my professional method of treatment."

"Ok." I said wondering what was number two.

"And" he said with a big pause before speaking again, " that you understand that your treatment will involve intensely physical contact between the two of us, up to and including orgasms."

My eyes flew open and I bolted upright on the sofa. Looking into Dr. Solomon's eyes I tried to see some hint that he was joking, but his eyes remained serious. "You say what?" I asked pretty sure I hadn't heard him right.

"That your treatment, as with the treatment of most of my patients will involve deeply sexual contact between you and myself."

Still blinking, I was speechless. When a question could form on my lips it was, "Did Val, I mean, did you?"

Without a pause and still looking completely confident and composed he responded by saying, "Valerie still continues her treatments at least twice a month."

"She does?" Was all my mouth could say as my mind raced ahead. What was he saying? Was Dr. Solomon just some kind of man ho, who charged two fifty a pop? If that was the case, as weak as it was I could get sex from Big Eric at home for free.

Then I thought about Val again and how amazing she was looking and feeling lately. Was this the reason she was still skipping to the loo every time I saw her? Could it be because the good Dr. Solomon was steady having sex 'therapy' with her twice a month?

He spoke and immediately brought me back to the matter at hand, "my concern right now Donna is you and your treatment. Please remember I am a professional and your sessions will be treated as such; so do we have an understanding?"

I thought about what he'd just said to me, and as shocked as I was, I tried to make some sense of what he was saying. I figured I could do one of two things. Either I could demand my money back and hurry up and hop back on the two buses and el train that would take me home; perhaps when I got home call Val and cuss her out for not putting me down with the fact that Dr. Solomon was a freak *or* I could ride with it at least this once and see what my hard earned money was going to get me with the tall dark skinned man in front of me.

Looking at Dr. Solomon while he patiently waited for my answer, I wondered what the hell this man could do to bring a smile like Val's to my face. Weighing my options, either go home in the cold feeling no better than when I first got here or find out what all the hype was about. I thought to myself 'what the hell' and decided to ride.

"Yes doctor, we have and understanding." I said thinking, 'this shit better be good!'

"Fantastic!" The doctor replied and for the first time a smile crept into his eyes making me think perhaps I made the right decision. "Now Donna, I need you to close your eyes again, keep them closed until I instruct you to open them, and as before I want you to breath deeply and relax."

I laid back down on the soft leather again, as I was told, but this time my deep breaths were followed by anticipation of what was to come next.

"The key to feeling whole," the doctor began while taking my feet into his hands removing my socks, "is by envisioning your own beauty, the deepest essence of your very being."

Saying nothing I continued breathing deeply.

"Become aware of very inch of yourself, from your head down to your toes, inside and out and give each centimeter the love and cherishing it deserves." He said while his hands caressed my feet, then his hands moved up my legs, stopping at my knees before cruising up my thighs, he then said, "The places my hands have touched, describe them for me." He said.

"My feet, my legs, my knees and my thighs." I answered, wishing I didn't have to talk; the feel of his hands was turning my stomach into jello.

"Yes, I know, but I'd like you to describe them, appreciatively describe them." He said his hands slowly making their way up to my inner thigh.

"I umm, have regular feet, size eight, with purple polish on my toe nails…" What was I supposed to say?

"You have beautiful feet," he said taking over the dialog; though I wouldn't say all that; "with pretty well groomed toes, delicate ankles and a high arched sole; they're like dancers feet, graceful and beautiful in their own right."

"Okay then…" I said but thinking, 'but damn doc, they're just feet.'

"Not just feet", he said and it was almost as if he could hear my thoughts. He continued, "they are the elegant extension of a magnificent body." Then Dr. Solomon surprised the hell out of me when he placed my right foot directly in his mouth, sucking on my toes and licking the sole and top of my foot. He gave the same attention to my left foot before speaking again, "they taste, smooth and delicious in my mouth" he said sucking on both big toes making them tickle like crazy. "In other words Donna, you have sexy feet." Then he made me repeat what he'd said using the same words like beautiful and sexy.

I was blown away, but what he did with my feet was nothing compared to what he did with every inch of my body as he moved about me, he removed whatever clothing was in that spot and then went about complimenting, kissing, caressing and loving every inch while describing that area, then asking me to follow up and do the same.

By the time I was down to my bra and panties, you couldn't tell me I didn't have the sexiest most beautiful, ears, elbows, arms, knees; you name it Dr. Solomon had me loving it.

When it came to my breast Dr. Solomon had me touch them myself and describe them to him. By now I was into the swing of my treatment and did the talking for him, "I have full, round juicy breasts, the swell of them is seductive, my skin is soft like satin, my nipples are firm and sensitive beneath my touch, I have pretty, sensual and sexy breast." I said smiling to myself, feeling really good about myself and my body, forgetting how many times in the past I told myself that I was too fat, my butt was too big, I looked too old; all the negative messages to myself slowly fading from my mind.

"So Donna, how are you feeling now?" He asked me.

"Good…no make that damn good." I said smiling with my eyes still closed.

"Great, than at this point I think your ready to take your treatment one step further." I heard him say.

"Ok that sounds good, what is the next step?" I asked still mentally flowing from the images of myself in my mind.

"Open you eyes Donna," I heard him say and when I did, hell I was glad I did. Dr Solomon had removed every piece of his clothing and stood over me on the sofa like he was ready to do some damage.

I took note of every inch of Dr. Solomon, and I could have sworn I was watching D'Angelo's video from back in the day. Doctor was long, lean and cut, and that smooth deep dark ran from his head all the way down to his toes. All I could think was, 'if this man ain't Zulu, I don't know who is!'

"Donna," he said, "Now I'm going to help you explore your inner beauty, the beauty deep inside." He said approaching me with a small foil packet in his right hand.

By now I'd been hanging out with the doctor for well over an hour and a half and was feeling pretty good up till this point. It wasn't till I peeked the condom in his hand did I the full impact of what was happening here register in my brain.

"Umm Doc, I don't know about this…" I said unsure.

Dr. Solomon stepped back a few steps making me more comfortable with the distance. "That's fine Donna, you've made a lot of progress today, if you want to stop here that's completely ok."

I watched him as he turned around to step back into his clothes and damn if his ass didn't look good too! Then I thought about my money and wondered why I was so quick to let him off so cheap, Dr. Solomon was obviously willing to do a whole lot more for his two hundred and fifty dollars; I'd be a fool not to let him. "Umm, no we can continue…I mean if it's alright with you."

When he turned back around the look on his face was serious, "Donna are you sure?"

"Yes, doctor I'm sure." I answered, sure that I was game to try whatever he had on the table at least.

With that Dr. Solomon moved back towards me on the couch and leaned in over me. With expert patience and skill he touched me in ever place that he missed earlier, his hands exploring everything in between, leaving a trail of warm tingling skin behind his touch.

Then without warning, he climbed between my legs and after sliding into protection he lifted me up by my thighs and plunged himself deeply and completely inside. Then he started talking to me again, this time describing how warm, wet, soft or tight I felt inside. Moving slowly, deliberately and with each motion making sure he kept a finger or a thumb toying against my clit.

By the time he sped up his pace, both of us were covered in sweat, but Dr. Solomon made sure I knew that this session was part of my therapy, he moaned and whispered one affirmation after another and had me repeat what he'd said.

When I felt a river of fire begin to swirl around between my legs, my head got dizzy and my legs went numb, but good old Dr. Solomon kept going never missing a beat. He didn't stop his stroke until I was completely done, though I noticed he never came himself.

By the time he was guiding me to the little bathroom outside his office I felt pretty much like I was floating on clouds. Looking in the mirror, I saw the person he'd spent over two hours telling me was there.

Instead of the plain, ordinary, down on her luck Donna, I saw the strong, beautiful, sensual and sexy Donna standing there before me. While splashing water on my face, I realized I'd been putting up with a whole lot in my life that I just didn't have to put up with; Big Eric for starters, when he got home tonight we were gonna have to have ourselves a talk. If he still loved me as much as I loved him, we were going to have to make some changes because I needed more from a marriage than what I had.

'Perhaps' I thought while still checking out the new me in the mirror, 'I should think about going back to school', I was only making the kind of money I made because I didn't know how to do anything else.

And to hell with that damn hooptie, right then I decided top take the bus while I worked on cleaning up my credit and saving up enough money for a down payment on a decent car.

Life was too short too waste I realized, and most if not all that was wrong in my life I had the power to change.

By the time I was fully dressed and heading out to the lobby there was a new patient waiting to be seen. Like me when I first got there, she sat like was a gray cloud hanging over her head.

Passing by her on my way out of the door I glanced at her giving her a smile and said "hello."

"What's it like?" She asked looking tense clutching the clipboard tightly in her hands.

"Girl, your gonna love your therapy. This was my first session and already it's changed my life!" I said bouncing out the door, ready to face the world.

The Party

Toni soaked her tired and sore muscles in a steaming tub deliciously scented with fragrant bath salts, still reeling from the events that took place earlier that evening.

Toni had moved to Philly only a few months before, her company promoted and relocated her from their Chicago location, to work in their marketing department as a Senior Market Analyst.

Work had been going good; she'd put in a lot of hours getting situated in her new environment. In the little time she'd been there she'd become key in implementing several new projects and so far each were going pretty well.

So well, that Toni had little time to think about being lonely at work; but alone in her new apartment, miles from her friends and family; Toni often felt the pangs of homesickness.

"Honey, have you tried getting out…meeting people?" Her mother asked in one of their daily conversations.

"I've really been busy Mom, but I will." Toni answered.

"I just don't like you being so far away, with no friends at all…" Her mother worried.

Toni was the youngest of four children, and though she was twenty-seven, her family still thought of her as the baby. Her mother was right on one account though; it was no fun being this far from home without even one person you could call a friend. Sure there were her new co-workers, but Toni could tell they were still trying to feel out the stranger from Chicago who nabbed the promotion they had all applied for. Most of them had already formed their own little cliques and they seemed reluctant to let Toni in, outside of their work environment.

Then she met Nycole, a lawyer who worked as a consultant in the legal department. The two met working out in the company gym, on the same schedule, every morning from six thirty to seven thirty.

Nycole was a vivacious petite powerhouse, full of adrenaline and conversation. She'd come to the gym amp'd every morning, smiling and chatting as if she'd just finished running a marathon. Just being around her was like drinking a double shot of espresso. Nycole even looked like fireworks. She was barely five foot two, with an impressively curvy figure; chin length head of reddish locks, cinnamon skin, full pretty lips and bright round eyes.

Unlike Toni who was at least four inches taller, a solid size ten, with pecan brown skin, shoulder length dark hair, slanted eyes and a pretty tilting mouth framed by dimpled cheeks.

It wasn't long before Toni found herself looking forward to seeing her each morning and was thrilled to find out they lived in the same Center City apartment building just off the Vine Street Expressway. In a short period of time they'd become fast friends, meeting for lunch, shopping for shoes after work, going to happy hour together.

It was one of those happy hours as they sipped pomegranate martinis at the Continental did Nycole ask Toni about her love life.

Taking another sip she asked, "So Toni, you dating anyone? Did you leave any broken hearts back in Chi Town?"

"I wish! I haven't so much as met a man outside of work since I've been here," Toni said shaking her head, "and I don't know, I'm not too comfortable with the online thing yet, especially being so new to the city."

"I hear you." Nycole asked looking interested.

"There was this one guy I was dating back in Chi, but I found out the hard way that he was married."

"What's the hard way?"

"One night we were leaving my apartment to head out for dinner, his wife pulled up and with one punch knocked him out on the ground then swung her hard ass fist at my head!" Toni said seriously.

"Oh God, what did you do?"

"First I ducked, then I knocked her ass out right there on top of her husband and left them both there." Toni said laughing.

"Damn, girl!" Nycole answered laughing so hard that she nearly spilled her drink. Then, "so what have you been doing to…you know, get off?"

Toni answered feeling good from her cocktail, "wearing the hell out of my little silver bullet; but to be honest, even that's starting to get a little old, if I don't meet someone soon, I may have to fly back to Chicago just for a booty call." Toni said half laughing, then she looked back at Nycole and asked, "what about you Nycole, do you have a boyfriend?"

"I don't have a boyfriend." Nycole answered.

"Oh, ok." That made sense to Toni; both of them were still young, not even thirty; so being single wasn't really that big of a deal.

"What I do have," Nycole continued, leaning in closer, "Is better than a boyfriend."

"What's better than a boyfriend?" Toni asked. The only thing that could beat one Toni guessed would be two.

"I have um…how should I put it; a support group." Nycole answered sipping on her bright red cocktail.

Toni didn't have a clue what she was talking about; perhaps Nycole misunderstood her, "no, I mean do you have a man?"

"Girl, I know what you meant the first time." She answered laughing. When she composed herself said, "Tell you what, if you're open minded, I'm having a little get together down at my place tomorrow. I want you to come by and meet my friends."

"Yeah, I'd love to come." Toni answered, excited about the idea of attending her first party in Philadelphia, forgetting that Nycole never really answered her question. "Should I bring anything, what should I wear?" She asked.

"Bring yourself and wear anything you want. You know me, I'll be in something comfortable and sexy."

"What time?" Toni asked.

"Round eightish."

"You're on."

That next evening Toni found herself down at Nycole's place, feeling sexy in a little black number and strappy red shoes. By the time she arrived at eight thirty there were at least a dozen people there already and more were coming in as she arrived.

Nycole's apartment was nice, very chic, and very contemporary. Her taste was modern and expensive. Toni recognized some of Nycole's furniture from her own future wish list. Like her cream Natuzzi leather sofa, suede chairs and matching suede ottoman. Every thing her eyes rested on was as fashionable as it was impressive.

Nycole herself looked just as she said, sexy and comfortable wearing a pair of white cotton gauze pants that sat low on her hips and swished gently as she walked, and a matching top that dipped low at her cleavage.

The atmosphere was lively but relaxed with the lights dimmed down to cocktail lighting. The music she played was mostly Soul and so was her food. Nycole had a spread of crispy chicken, spicy jerk turkey, seasoned greens, a jumbo shrimp salad, savory beans and rice, corn bread and a tossed salad; and it all looked delicious. Toni was going have to put in double time at the gym by the time she finished sampling it all.

Her guests were just as lively, it was early in the evening but already everyone was talking, laughing and enjoying themselves. There was a card game going on one of the corners and on the other side of the room a line dance had started to form. This gathering was very much like it was for her getting together with her friends and family back home, Toni immediately felt like she fit in.

Throughout the night she easily mingled, gliding up to one group of people chatting for a while before moving on again; she even stopped to do a few line dances before heading to the sumptuous spread. When she spotted Nycole passing out cups of mixed cocktails, she'd already sampled several small plates of food and was now nibbling on chicken, greens and cornbread. She gave Nycole a smile and a nod letting her know, that everything was so good and she was having a ball.

"Having a good time girl?" Nycole asked her while making her rounds around the room

"Yeah, this party is really cool." Toni said accepting a drink. "And your food is banging!"

"Thank you girl," Nycole said then looking over Toni's shoulder said, "I have someone I want you to meet."

Toni turned around to face the finest hunk of man she'd ever laid eyes on. He was tall, chocolate and with the whitest, brightest smiled she'd ever seen. 'well hello Clark Dark,' she thought while Nycole made introductions.

"Toni this is Desmond, he's from my group…Des, this is Toni, she's the new girl at work I was telling you about."

"Hello Toni," Desmond said taking her hand, "I heard a lot about you." Desmond's voice had a beautiful lilting accent, something African, perhaps Nigerian, Toni thought.

"A lot about me?" Toni said surprised.

"Yeah, Nycole said you can really get your work out on," Desmond said then eyeing her from top to bottom said, "and I've got to say it has definitely paid off…"

Toni responded with a quick "thank you" and a blush. She wanted to tell him he looked just as good, maybe better, but the cat got her tongue.

"Girl, pay Des no mind, he's just a big flirt." Nycole said waving her hand.

Desmond grabbed Nycole playfully around her waist and pulled her close to him. "That's all I am?" Desmond asked.

"Boy, get outta here!" Nycole replied slapping his hands away and laughing.

Desmond planted a huge kiss on her cheek and one on Toni's hand before excusing himself. "Glad I met you Toni." He said with a wink, just before another guest caught his eye and he moved on.

"Whew, that man is fine!" Nycole said fanning herself.

"Yeah he is!" Toni said instantly taken with him. She was hoping she'd get a chance to talk with him again before the night was over.

"And..." Nycole continued, "he has a stroke that can make a woman's toes curl, while she speaks in tongues, if you know what I mean."

"Oh," Toni said, understanding completely. Toni thought that she should have known a man as gorgeous as Desmond was taken, but then Toni was confused, if she remembered correctly, Nycole said she didn't have a man.

She mentioned that 'group' again, Toni meant to ask her to elaborate yesterday at the Continental, but it slipped her mind. Before the question could form in her mind again, Nycole took her by the hand and was guiding her towards a couple that had just arrived. "Carrie, Trey, I'd like you to meet Toni" Nycole offered.

Toni took in the married couple as Nycole finished the introduction. Carrie and Trey looked to be in their mid to late thirties, Carrie could even be forty. Both were attractive enough, Trey had a café au lait complexion with a head of dark curls that were beginning to gray slightly at the temples and a sleek dark mustache above his lip. He looked to be in pretty good shape, not as tall as Desmond but built nicely just as well; Toni wondered if he ever played football, with such well-defined arms.

Carrie was several inches taller than Trey, slender almost skinny. Taking in her facial features, Toni immediately thought of the singer Sade, though Carrie's skin was several shades darker; her smooth features blending together nicely with her deep caramel skin.

"Nice to meet you both," Toni said.

Nycole told her a little about them, Trey was a sports reporter and wrote a column for the local paper and Carrie was a city schoolteacher.

"So Toni, Nycole tells us you're from Chicago", Carrie began.

"Uh, yeah I am." Toni answered, wondering how many more people at the party knew who she was and where she'd come from.

"If I knew there were beautiful women like you in Chicago, I would have gone there for more than the Bears and deep dish pizza." Trey said laughing.

Toni, not sure how to respond said nothing, she simple observed Carrie's expression and realized Carrie didn't seem to be fazed by her husband's comment. "I bet you would have," Carrie said, "perhaps I would have joined you." Carrie said taking in Toni's body as hard as her husband had just done.

'Ain't that some…' Toni began thinking to herself, but her thought was interrupted when a woman, not much older than herself joined the four of them. This girl, in her short yellow dress was nothing less than stunning, Toni thought, suddenly feeling not as sexy in the presence of this girl.

She was a medium brown with flawless skin, large round brown eyes, smooth black hair, satiny black eyebrows and lashes to match. She had a shape that could easily rival the hottest video vixen out there; thick but completely fit and a set of flawless strong legs to boot.

"This is our girl Melani," Nycole said, seeming to stand half of Melani's height. When Melani spoke, her voice was light and soft almost like a little girl's. While they exchanged handshakes Desmond rejoined them making the little circle a total of six people. "And this" Nycole, said gesturing to the circle, "is our little group."

Toni looked around still rather confused, "what kind of group?"

Carrie spoke up first, " a pleasure support' group."

"Swingers?" Toni said finally understanding what was going on here.

"I guess that's somewhat correct," Trey added, "except we're exclusive to each other."

"What does that mean?" Toni asked feeling a little worried; did Nycole set her up for some kind of gangbang? She looked around the room there were other people there still enjoying themselves, none of them were privy to the conversation she was having with Nycole and her friends.

Melani chimed in next, "that means were all each other's lovers either as a group; which is my favorite; or separately. We take care of each other."

"This is what I was trying to tell you last night," Nycole added. "I'm not interested in a one on one relationship right now, dating is kinda out of the question, my schedule is way too busy, but I get horny just like anyone else. I'm not into bed hopping either so when Carrie, Trey and Desmond approached me about a year ago, it was like the answer to my dilemma."

"Then came me," Melani said, "I'm the newbie, and I was approached maybe five months ago."

This was as about as freaky a conversation as Toni had ever had. She wasn't naïve, she knew there were people who were into stuff like this, though she'd never met any personally. "Approached you, like your approaching me now?"

"Yes", Nycole began. "I like you, and we thought that maybe you'd enjoy being in a group like ours. Were all about love, freedom, respect and trust."

"None of us are expected to do anything we don't' want to do, but on the other hand were happy to please each other in any way we can." Melani added.

"For someone who likes fun with no strings attached, it's the perfect relationship; we have the best of all worlds. We are all disease free, drug free and faithful to each other, but totally free to live our lives as well. Anything or anyone you'd want to do is fine as long as it's with someone from the group, but no one takes possession or ownership of anyone else." Nycole said, getting nods and words of agreement from each of them as she spoke.

Toni looked around; true she sometimes was lonely and horny, and just as true she really wasn't looking for everlasting love right now, but she didn't even know what these people were into. There were two guys, and already three women. Who was going to be with whom? All of this was way too freaky for her. She suddenly felt claustrophobic and was just about to tell Nycole she had to leave and get the hell out of there when Desmond spoke up.

"You would of course, be in very, very good hands Toni," He said taking her hand into his, "I'll make sure of it." His accent making her melt.

"Tell you what", Nycole continued, "my party will be clearing out soon and the five of us are going to take our own party into my bedroom. If you're interested let yourself in and join us. If not, no problem you and I are cool no matter what." With that she pressed a gold key hanging from a heart shaped fob into Toni's left palm.

Toni grabbed her purse and excused herself. Barely saying goodbyes she left Nycole's apartment as quickly as she could. Riding the elevator up to her floor she didn't realized she'd been clutching the key fob so tightly that, there was a heart shaped imprint pressed into her hand.

Reaching her apartment, Toni shut the door and let out a long sigh. Not even bothering to turn the lights on she headed to her bedroom and started to undress.

This had been the craziest night of her life; who would have thought that cool down to earth Nycole was into something as wild as a swingers group.

And what in the world made Nycole think she would be down with something like that. Sure she was alone in a new city, sure she hadn't had any for months even before she moved to Philly, but that didn't mean she was up to getting involved in an all out orgy.

Toni laid in her bed squeezing her eyes shut, trying to force herself to go to sleep; trying to block out the conversation she'd just had with Nycole and her friends. The harder she tried to keep her eyes shut the more her mind replayed what was said to her.

She thought about Carrie and Trey and how different they were from the married guy she'd dated in Chicago and his wife. There was no anger or violence between them, even as Trey was obviously coming on to her. Trey got to mess around with his wife's permission and from what Carrie was saying, she was probably into girls as well.

Then there was Nycole and Melani, both really hot women, if nothing else Toni was curious to see what they would look like, what they would do in a sexual setting.

Finally her mind came to Desmond, he had to be the most beautiful man she'd ever come across; he easily looked as if he could handle three women, four if she had agreed to join them.

The image of Desmond is what sent her mind into motion. She tried picturing him taking, Nycole or Melani or even Carrie into his long arms and making love to them. He mind strained to create images and scenarios of them all kissing, touching and pleasing each other.

Still thinking, she slipped her hand under her pillow and pulled out her silver bullet, turning it on she slid it between her legs and began her routine of pleasing herself. It felt good, as she slid the tiny vibrating egg over her shaved smoothness to her hooded clitoris. Wetting the tip of her finger with her tongue she made the area moist as she continued rubbing the silver egg all across her lips.

Throwing her head back she enjoyed the sensation as her hips slowly ground against her hands and the egg. She pictured herself with the five of them, trying things she was even too afraid to think about.

Then she let her mind wander to both men, what would it feel like to experience both of them at the same time, what would it be like to have one inside her mouth while the other was between her legs.

Toni was getting so aroused from her thoughts that she began feeling dizzy right there in her bed, when the room began to spin she realized it was from her own powerful orgasm. Sliding her fingers deep inside she rode her fingers through one pulsating wave into the other. Her body shuddered so hard as she crested that she cried out loud, moving her fingers feverishly until she hit the last wave.

"Damn!" She said to herself in the darkness, "why in the world am I up here alone doing this, when the opportunity of a lifetime is just four floors down". Opening her eyes she looked over to her nightstand. There the heart shaped key fob gleamed in the moonlight filtering in from her window. Toni had planned to return it to Nycole at work on Monday, but now she knew more than anything she wanted to use that key tonight.

Jumping out of bed, she quickly freshened up in the bathroom. After oiling her body down and touching up her makeup, she rummaged through her lingerie drawer and came upon a seductive jewel green and black lace bra and matching black thong. Sliding back into her black dress and shoes, Toni was headed out the door.

Four flights down Toni was turning the key into the door of Nycole's apartment; her heart beating like a drum inside her chest. The apartment was now dark, the dozens of people had long since left. The only sounds she heard were quiet moans coming from Nycole's bedroom.

Toni tiptoed down the hall, not wanting her presence to yet be discovered. Slowly opening the door Toni stopped short once she saw what going on inside. The view from the door knocked her senses to the floor. Only Nycole noticed her standing there and greeted her with a silent smile.

The five of them were all on Nycole's king sized bed, her black silk sheets gathered and twisted all beneath them, their bodies bathed in candlelight. Carrie was at the head of the bed, her head thrown back and her legs spread wide as Melani hungrily licked and sucked her. Behind Melani was Trey taking her from behind working his muscular thighs and ass as he plowed himself hard against her round bottom.

Next to them was Nycole and Desmond in a sixty-nine, Desmond on the bottom with his tongue extended deep into Nycole and Nycole on top managing to take most of Desmond's massive length.

Toni was frozen there at the door, only half believing what her eyes saw, it was beyond her comprehension that all this debauchery was taking place right before her eyes, the sounds alone taking over her senses, completely intoxicating her.

Nycole's loud slurping sounds as she tried to swallow more of Desmond, Melani's soft wet kissing sounds as she satisfied Carrie, Carrie's groans of pleasure, Trey breathing deeply uttering Melani's name as he slid back and forth inside her, Desmond whispering dirty words as his mouth sucked and pulled on Nycole's box.

Still at the door, Toni slipped her hand inside her panties as she watched Carrie begin to tremble from cumming. Carrie locked her fingers into Melani's hair and brought her face tightly against her. Melani wrapped her arms around Carrie's thighs lifting her hips off the bed and burying her face in even deeper.

Carrie's back arched even farther, her small breast bouncing as Melani pulled her back and forth against her mouth, then screaming wildly she came.

From there they fell in sequence, Desmond grunting loudly as he shot load upon load into Nycole's waiting mouth. Nycole had lifted her head and extended her tongue while gazing into Toni's eyes as Desmond shot endless ribbons of cream on her waiting tongue.

Toni gazed back knowing Nycole's performance was for her benefit, Desmond was what brought her here and Nycole was kind enough to let her know what she was in store for.

Then Nycole's eyes squeezed shut as Desmond took her over the edge, she lifted her body now sitting directly on his face, moaning as she rocked back and forth across his tongue cumming hard.

Next Melani starting crying in her soft fuck me voice, "Mmm Carrie your husband is fucking me so damn good!" and he was, he had pulled Melani up on his lap and with his strong arms lifted her whole weight up and down on his hardness, holding her tight as she trembled in her own orgasm.

When she was through, Melani climbed off and then covered him with her mouth, followed by his wife who licked his sack gently while Melani licked up and down his length. Trey was moaning saying both his wife and Melani's names low and deep. He almost growled as he came deep in Melani's mouth holding her head firmly until the very last second. Melani lifted her head and with a smile passed his gift onto Carrie through a kiss.

Toni was overwhelmed with what she'd just witnessed. A whole lot had taken place before her, some of she was willing to try and some she really wasn't. Watching as everyone rose from the bed she wondered how they would feel about her not wanting to be with women, would they still want her to join their group?

"Soo, what do think?" Nycole asked walking up to her naked, skin moist with sweat, her bright eyes looking calm and relaxed.

Toni was speechless for several moments, when she was able to speak her words stammered out, "I don't know what to say," she said bashfully.

"Say you want to join us." Desmond said, he and the others now standing closely around her, only Carrie and Melani bothering to cover themselves with robes.

Toni looked at all of them; sex and sensuality pouring from all of them. Finally her gaze rested on Desmond, he stood in front of her naked and magnificent. Without thinking for another second she knew what her answer would be. "Yes, I want to join you."

"That a girl!" Desmond replied giving her a hug, then each of them following suit. Carrie hugged her the longest placing a soft wet kiss on her cheek. To her own surprise she didn't pull away.

Then Nycole and Melani took Toni by the hand leading her toward the bed, helping her remove her clothes as she walked. By the time she reached the bed, she was naked of everything except her bra and panties. Trey and Desmond did her the honors then, Trey removing her bra from behind her and Desmond tugging on her panties down to her ankles allowing her to step out of them.

The other women now watching as Trey and Desmond toyed and fingered Toni began touching and rubbing each other casually. As Desmond led Toni onto the bed, everyone followed watching intently as Toni returned both Desmond's and Trey's kisses.

Soon, Toni found herself laying on her back in the center of the bed, a man on each side of her and both of her hands filled with their newly rising hard ons while each man fondled and kissed her alternately. The women followed rubbing and kissing all over her arms, legs, belly, hands and feet.

Toni looked around, concerned with who was doing what to her, worried that both men and women were touching her. She was ok with Trey and Desmond but not so sure about Melani, Nycole and Carrie. Before she could protest, Trey covered her mouth with his and kissed her deeply. As he did she felt two mouths close around her nipples and begin sucking softly, and another mouth kiss the smoothness of her belly.

A million thoughts began swirling around in her mind, for a moment she wondered why she came here…why she agreed to let this happen? What did it say about her that not only two men were touching and caressing her naked body, but also there were two women happily sucking on her breast and one more was now tongue kissing her navel. What would her friends and family think if they saw here now, for sure her mother would freak out if she knew.

She was feeling anxious and overwhelmed with all the attention she was receiving along with the mental tug of war of whether this was wrong or right. As hard as she tried to relax, her body remained tense; the fact that having her body kissed, touched and caressed by so many at one time felt completely amazing escaped her.

The hotter her body became though, the more she realized it didn't really matter what anyone else thought about it…at least not at this moment. No one but the people in the room with her had to know what she was up to; no one would know her secret unless she decided to tell it. In her mind Toni decided to enjoy what she was experiencing if nothing else then for experimentation; and if enjoying all this pleasure was wrong, she'd just have to be wrong then.

Toni took in a deep ragged breath, closed her eyes and just allowed herself to feel the pleasure she was receiving. Before long she began to easily respond to the sensations, her body to relaxing her breath panting softly.

Opening her eyes she saw Desmond, as he crawled between her legs and began tasting her and Trey as he brought his hard-on to her face. Without hesitation, Toni let him slip between her lips and drew him in and out gently.

Nycole still sucking on her left nipple had reached one hand down behind Desmond's head and was guiding his face harder between her Toni's legs.

Toni began moaning softly with Trey still in her mouth as Melani continued to lick and suck her right nipple, cupping in her hand and she sucked. Toni could see her but she knew it was Carrie who was kissing and caressing her belly and thighs very close to where Desmond licked and slurped between her legs loudly.

When Desmond let a groan, the women instinctively moved so that he could take over her body. Toni shifted with him removing Trey from her mouth only long enough to turn her body around as Desmond drew her up on her knees.

Toni returned Trey to her mouth just as Desmond entered her but released him just as quickly to gasp from the size of what was being forced into her. Desmond patiently waited for Toni's body to respond to him and when it did he increased his speed to a steady rhythm.

Toni could not believe how good Desmond felt inside her, each time she thought she'd taken all of him, he moved forward offering her more. Desmond whispered to her as he moved inside her, his African accent driving her crazy. Toni only wished she could see his handsome face as he spoke.

Melani moving to the side of the bed, entertained herself with Nycole once more but Carrie kept her attention fixed on Toni, rubbing her back and her swaying breast as they moved back and forth from Desmond's strokes.

Soon Trey took Carrie and in the same position moved his wife's body to the beat the couple beside them, matching their rhythm beat for beat.

Toni glanced to her left, watching in interest as husband and wife made love to each other. Trey held his wife tightly grinding his hips into her, Carrie's eyes were closed shut in concentration as she received her husband, whispering to her husband how much she loved him.

To her right was Nycole and Melani, Nycole's face was almost completely covered by her reddish locks the only expression Toni could see on her face was her mouth wide open as she moaned "Ohh" with each bob of Melani's head between her legs. Though not ready to try it herself, Toni had to admit that watching the two women together was a very, very sensual experience.

Toni curved her back further, letting herself take in more of Desmond, now whispering back to him, letting him know how much she loved the way he was making her feel.

Toni couldn't believe she was there, in the middle of all of them and as kinky and raunchy as she considered it to be, she loved every single second of it. The sounds, the scents, the sights...all of it turned her on. Sure she wanted a one on one love one day, but until that day came she knew she could do a lot worse than having five sexy friends, all who liked to take cater to each other's physical desires.

Toni was now number six in what Carrie called a 'pleasure support group', and if this was what it was like to belong to an exclusive swingers group, she was more than happy to be a member. Toni was hooked and she wanted more. The next thing on her agenda was to sample Trey and find out what those strong arms would feel like wrapped around her.

This time Toni was the first to scream from satisfaction. Desmond smiled while watching Toni's back as she jerked against him, the sound of her cries turning the rest on so much that they all came in succession one after another.

The force in which Desmond came inside her shocked her, especially after she'd seen him release such a huge load earlier. He held her tightly still whispering in her ear until the last pulsation rushed between her aching legs.

When they all laid there finally spent and satisfied, Nycole curled up at the head of her bed, Melani already falling asleep not far from her towards the foot of the bed, with some of the sheets pulled up to her waist. Trey laid on her other side of her spooned up with his wife both looking tired and content seconds away from falling asleep as well. Finally, Toni laid on her side there in the middle cradled in Desmond's long arms, as he kissed the well of her neck softly.

Nycole was the only person to speak, "So Toni girl," She said with a yawn, her relaxed voice just above a whisper, "this was your first time with the support group…will it be your last?" She asked, smiling knowing the answer.

"No girl," she said stretching, wrapping her arms around Desmond getting comfortable in his embrace, " I think you've got yourself a permanent addition, I wanna be a member for life!"

Acknowledgements

Well, its kinda hard thanking the people who inspired me to write 'Hot Like Fire' without putting their personal business on blast. But you know who you are, and thank you for sharing your secrets.

Sex lies at the root of life, and we can never learn to reverence life until we know how to understand sex.
Henry Ellis

Good sex is like good bridge. If you don't have a good partner, you'd better have a good hand.
Mae West

There's more to love than just sex, and romance alone will eventually become boring, but put the two together and damn if they don't make a hell of a combination!
Leah Lockett Harris

Leah Lockett Harris, a native of Philadelphia, she now resides with her husband and two children in Cherry Hill, NJ.

If you enjoyed 'Hot Like Fire', try my first novel
'Delicious'

Distribution by LuLu.com 626571
ISBN 978-0-6151-4038-4

available now

stay tuned for more books by
Leah Lockett Harris

www.ingramcontent.com/pod-product-compliance
Lightning Source LLC
Chambersburg PA
CBHW051754040426
42446CB00007B/367